'You did an Eat, Pray, Runaway and Return,' someone once quipped.

True story ….

A Grown Up's Gap Year

The Guidebook for Mid Lifestyle. Wellbeing. Adventure. Chic.
'...put You in the picture.'

Monique van Tulder

Editor: Melinda Louise Hutchings – www.melindalouisemedia.com

Text & Design Concept: Monique van Tulder

Cover Design, Artwork & Illustrations: Madeleine Carroll

Published in 2025 by Monique van Tulder and Clark & Mackay

CLARK & MACKAY

Love and Gratitude

To anyone who stopped in their day to read words I've written.

To My Loves

Husband Michael, for being 'the one', sons Benjamin and Henry, for bringing the colour to my life, and meaning to all that I am.

Cornelia and Reinier, my mum and dad. For your zest for life and being my champions.

Sister Michelle, for giving me a loving push, to back myself.

Without you all, I may have missed the signpost to an expanded journey.

A story that begins with you.

This isn't a guidebook on how to ditch your life and jet off to a tropical island (though let's be honest, that's tempting). It's about rediscovering your spark, feeling better, joyful seeking, and putting you in the picture.

A big hug for you in mid-life.

And if that involves a temporary escape? Well, who am I to judge?

Welcome to A Grown Up's Gap Year –

a journey you won't want to miss.

Monique xx

CONTENTS

For The Record
The Time Mum Got Mad And Took Off
How To Use This Guidebook

THE JOURNEY BEGINS 31
The Four Seasons Of Mid-Life
Create Space In Four Seasons Of Mid-Life
A Grown Up's Gap Year In A Nutshell
You Are Your 'Now' Project
Begin Here Tomorrow Morning
How Did We Get Here?
A Few Things To Get Off Our Chest
Begin At The End, Then Add Yes
What I Wish Someone Had Told Me
Listening to Wisdom

WINTER – FEEL EMPOWERED..............71
Be The Star Of Your Own Show
Your Mid-Life Journey Quiz
Invisible? Irrelevant? Absolutely Not!
Embracing Possibility
Hello Hindsight
Start Streamlining Your Lifestyle
Anxiety Expert Dr Danielle Einstein
How To (Start To) Feel Reinvigorated
Motherlode And Finances
Finance Expert Melissa Browne
Property Expert Michelle Van Tulder
Why, What, How – The Roadmap
Discovering Confidence

SPRING – FEEL REINVIGORATED........137
A Healthy Daily Practice Is Freeing
Understanding the Secret of Feeling Better
No-One Knows Your Body Better Than You
Menopause Insight Shelly Horton

The Power of Doing Less
Mindfulness Expert Kate Kendall
Setting Up to Be a Sleep Slayer
The Wellness vs Wellbeing Malarkey
Eating in Mid-Life Made Simple
That Daily Food Plan You Mentioned?
Recipe: Omelette
Moving in Mid-Life
Integrative Health Expert Sally-Ann Cowen
Mid-Life Maintenance Mojo
Skincare Expert Dr Michelle Squire
Just Wear the Bikini

SUMMER – FEEL ADVENTUROUS......225
A Grown Up's Gap Year Cautionary Tale
The Folly of Running Away
Going It Alone
Do Extraordinary Things, Anywhere
Amazing Women Doing Interesting Things
Ideas for a Grown Up's Gap Year
Wellness Expert Lisa Manser
Why I am a Fan of Wellbeing Retreats

AUTUMN – FEEL CONNECTED..........291
Returning Home
'Til Mid-Life Do Us Part, or Not
Relationship Expert Lissy Abrahams
Goodbyes and All That Entails
Sex in Mid-Life
Feeling Connected
Navigating a (Still) Full House
My Parenting Advice?
The Joy Found in Lending a Hand
The Elixir of Youth
An Open Mind is Interesting and Engaging
Career in Mid-Life

DESTINATION, YOUR MID-LIFE........333
There is No One Path
The Treasure in Your Backyard
Wrapping Up a Grown Up's Gap Year
If All Else Fails … Pavlova Recipe

Final Checklist
Book Club Questions

I believe we have strayed far from what is truly important – community, a sense of curiosity, our creativity, time in nature to nurture body and soul – all with an adventurous spirit. Our current lifestyle may as well be in outer space for all it might resemble the plans we had for our trajectory.

Now it's time to seek your joy, fulfil your dreams!

Monique xx

For The Record

- I am a health and wellbeing advocate; an asthmatic childhood, thyroid cancer in my twenties, and the birth of health-compromised sons led me to leave a management career in hotels and airlines and retrain in a lifelong passion – health and wellbeing. I am a certified health & wellness coach, nutritionist, fitness trainer, and cookbook, travel, and lifestyle writer.

- I am also a mum, wife, daughter, sister, and friend. When this book called for an opinion in these spheres, I've offered mine – naturally, your view will be unique, so take on board what resonates with you and let the rest go.

- I am not a medical professional, relationship counsellor, dietician, financial or property adviser, or psychiatrist – I defer to the professionals in their field. I've interviewed, questioned, listened, read, and then added my practical knowledge and responses.

- I've quoted and named with permission. Scientific papers, personal anecdotes, and studies cited are referenced by name on my website, where you will find other free resources, recipes, book lists – a mid-life survival kit of information.

- I hope I've achieved a flow for you in the manner intended – with measure afforded to evidence, along with my story, leaving ample room for you to add yours. For, in your life, you remain the expert.

Throughout the book, you'll see margin notes like this one. They vary from my repartee to recommendations. Unless otherwise stated, the resources mentioned in these margin notes can be found on my website.

A Premise of Sorts

Journey
noun: something suggesting travel or passage from one place to another.
verb: to go somewhere.

Someone may have told me (I certainly didn't listen), that mid-life might come with a side of quiet rebellion. That one day you could wake up with a suitcase packed and the dog wondering if they're coming too.

I'll confess, I resisted the label 'mid-life', ensuring a 50th birthday came and went with little to no fanfare. A few years passed amid a household stacked to the rafters with hormones. In hindsight my peri-menopause symptoms hovered for years – with no expression at the time I'd put the 'feels' down to hot summer nights, an irritating husband bouncing around in a euphoric career renaissance, and teen sons. Then end of school life for the youngest, my professional life in the loo – a sense of 'what the hell is going on', and, is 'this it'?

Something shifted – with it, a sense of whooshing time.

Seemingly overnight, the sinking realisation that I was 54 years old and remained at the top of everyone's 'people we need' pyramid and the bottom of my own. No surprise then that one morning I woke with a yearning for space. Figuratively and literally. I dreamt of soaring. Of my own expanse. Resilience (always my safety net) – well, she was nowhere to be found.

At first, I figured a stern self-talk and a brisk jog would snap me back. Nope. I started looking around, convinced I was missing something. Still, no clue. The feelings kept piling up until I barely recognised myself. No-one seemed to grasp it when I said I'd hit my limit – truth be told, I probably didn't have the words to articulate how drained I was.

'Untethered-you is a dangerous state,' said sister Michelle, my sage and caution. She was correct. I was utterly without direction. Sad, sweaty, feeling passed over, and perpetually pissed off.

With this in mind, I eventually did what any self-respecting middle-aged woman would do – I ran away from my husband, my kids, my mum, even our sweet puppy. First a few thousand kilometres; I left to change lightbulbs in an interstate home and stayed for five months. Then I booked a trip two continents away. I jumped off cliffs (literally), pondered how to simplify my life, and contemplated my 'next bit'. I needed to discover if I still had it, an edge, if there was more to me than the weight of everyone else's needs on my shoulders.

My family calls it 'the time Mum got mad and took off'. I prefer to think of it as my great awakening.

The Time Mum Got Mad and Took Off

Displeasure stimulating and focusing – so, too, milestones and tragedy. The icing on the shitstorm sandwich? Learning of the death of a childhood pal and once-ago love – part of my forever landscape, until he wasn't.

I believe there is a capacity for which the human spirit can continue to endure. Events can steer the course of life, with little regard for preferences. People cope. Then a saturation point. When one more thing – not necessarily worse than the others – becomes the tipping point. It eventually dawned I had two choices: wallow in self-pity and spend the ensuing decades trudging a gentle path toward death pissed off at my lot or honour my good fortune with a rediscovery of my zest. I chose the latter, yearning to ditch the sepia for a life back in technicolour.

A roof over our heads, love, health, family and friends, and life.

The precise moment I decided to 'bolt'? Much later I concluded it was the sum of the preceding five decades. All paths leading to the morning I found myself on a drive I had taken a thousand times before, along the familiar curves of a narrow stretch of road hugging the pristine coastline from the seaside township of Airlie Beach in the Whitsundays to our family holiday house. It's a region that serves many memories. The last place I had 'lived at home', the first place I had a job in what would become my professional life, my 21st birthday, schoolies week, the place I crawled to at 19 years old when life had already dealt too many blows, buying a forever home with a newborn in arms, and then years of holidays with my sons, husband, and Mum. The place I left behind in search of new horizons – and now to where I escaped. I returned after a COVID-length absence. Then I stayed.

The Whitsundays is in North Queensland, Australia.

Playing Hooky

Diary Note:

First morning. Something feels different. Perhaps the result of an unbroken sleep (it's been a while since I've felt refreshed and actually bounded out of bed). Perhaps waking without a packed agenda for one and all. Resisting the urge to check my phone, I sit with a frisson of excitement – a long time since I could articulate this sentiment. Coffee in hand, listening to calling curlew, the squawk of a cockatoo, trade winds rustling bushland. Watching the tide turn in the bay, sun rising with ribbons of peach and orange and pink – such intensity as if to be entirely made up. A sense of adventure awaiting.

As I drove to town, I glanced out the window and felt compelled to stop the car. Across the harbour, sea glistening, a few yachts made their way between the islands. A distant memory of a boyfriend asking me to sail with him to Bali, another wanting a life of perpetual winter in ski resorts, the carelessness with which I dismissed these suggestions at the time (running away is how I saw it – while I had a career to build, roots to lay down). I wondered when on earth I'd adopted the mantle of doing little that floats my boat – instead a life of keeping everyone else afloat. In that split second, a sense of coming home – I am a grown-up; not every decision requires a committee. Hubby is happy with his lot, my children are young adults – I can make decisions for myself, again.

Ten minutes later I found myself in the post office registering for a local PO box. Then a short note to the family – 'here is where I can now be found' – I switched off my phone for the remainder of the day and settled into the sense of playing hooky … from my life. Feeling brave, and apprehensive, because, to the best of my knowledge, this is not what committed mums and wives do – flee. I know my contentment is my responsibility – a choice, a gift I'm determined not to waste. So, while joy has gone missing, I'm going looking. I read today that an oak tree doesn't produce acorns until it is 50 years old … this feels like a nudge from the universe. Sure, life's only certainty is its unpredictability, but for now, being here feels right. Who knows what tomorrow will bring? Let's be honest, this is a far cry from the past 20 years of full shopping trolleys and a mind crammed with everything for everyone else. So, I can be found here, for a bit. The decision to stay organic. Sort of.

How did I get here? You might recognise the trope.

Mums in my sphere shoulder the bulk of family manoeuvres – still. Despite the different shapes families now inhabit, most of the time it's mum upon whom the majority of child-rearing falls. A caveat: I am aware that having offspring, family, and friends to love is a privilege. My sons, their dad, my parents, and my sisters (though I'm having a mini sibling hiatus from one right now, we will make up, eventually) are the best part of my life; individually and collectively they were not the catalyst for my departure.

It was parenting as a verb for 20 years (honestly, why did this become 'de rigueur' – are our kids better off for the stuff, the hovering, the never-a-minute-to-just-be lifestyles we have thrust them into? I'm arguing no). Frankly it wasn't the 'doing' that wore me out – it was the relentless mental juggling of everyone else's needs. Taking on my role of Chief of Staff of family life and overseer of domestic minutiae a gradual slide of circumstance, practicality, and necessity. COVID only intensified this, trapping our two teenage sons in a bubble of forced dependence when they could have been spreading their wings. Like everyone else, prolonged time in close quarters with little outside interaction became detrimental to 'family health'.

See the chapter 'Parenting as a Verb: The Hand We Have Played in Messing Up Our Kids'.

If I'm being entirely honest, also a situation of my own making. At the forefront of any scenario, tambourine in hand, smoothing the way for others – default 'performing seal', ensuring everyone's comfort. A yes person (you too probably recognise the battle cry: 'yes, of course I will'). Underneath it all, though, I crave solitude. In a bustling household, dreaming of a quiet corner where I can retreat. Forget Virginia Woolf's *A Room of One's Own* – I'd settle for a peaceful cupboard, preferably with a lock on the inside – instead, a few daily peaceful moments in the loo.

Mid-life comes with shifting sands – children leaving the nest (or staying), relationships may have run their course, careers sputtering. With it, a sense of '... is this all there is'? Overwhelm was my first thought: 'How do I even start to change things?' It's not easy to alter patterns of decades.

Standing in front of the mirror, I barely recognised the slightly pudgy, sluggish woman staring back. All I wanted to do was lie down under my doona and tell the world to piss off – for a bit.

Yes, we could throw our hands up as we age, attributing physical and mental decline to 'getting older', possibilities seemingly shrinking, yet an expanded life, vitality – vim and vigour – these are ageless attributes. Health issues aside, cultivating 'V & V' is not beyond most of us. If variety (and a bit of effort) is the spice of life, then vitality is the gift you'll receive in spades.

Spoiler alert

Eventually I returned, and began to write, I'd thought a nice travelogue about how to retreat / getaway should do the trick. I'd throw in a little packing advice (upfront – take out three quarters, it will still be plenty), list a slew of gorgeous locations where no one will find you (from your local beach to the European Alps – both fine choices).

Except having been away, done all that – I returned to an unanswered question. How to bring home the sense of contentment that had settled, the feeling of wellbeing, rude good health, coming back to myself, creativity for my future, simplicity via a less is more approach, back to the fundamentals, and yes, that overused word with all its current commercially driven connotation: 'wellness'. Harbouring some hope the moment the plane's wheels touched down at Sydney's Kingsford Smith Airport the tarmac would reveal a metaphorical red carpet. The road to omniscience. Well, I was in for a rude shock when the dust settled – Still. No. Bloody. Blueprint. That's when I set about reinvigorating every aspect of my life – I had health and fitness in the bag, the rest also needed an overhaul.

A Grown Up's Gap Year came to be – and the travel guide became a mid-lifestyle guidebook, because at some point, I realised I wasn't the only one feeling like this. Countless women shared just how confounded, bamboozled, and downright perplexed they felt by this stage of life. The magic in shared stories, collective shape -shifting, that's what this is all about. And frankly, one of the most delicious things you will encounter on this journey (yes, we will use that word, many times over). Because whilst wild ride, trip, roadmap, all have their place – journey is what this really is. We're in it together, travelling from one place to another – physically and mentally. I fervently believe sitting with yourself, holding your own hand, should be a mid-life rite of passage, to get out of your own way to create space, reshape your lifestyle, and contemplate your second (and yes third) acts. I am also convinced that, if the yearning to leave strikes, you are not dreaming of the gold at the end of the rainbow. You simply need to go away to breathe. You might have a great life – so it is not about finding a better one. Plain and simple – it is about rediscovering you. And then returning restored and ready to engage in your life, on your terms – better equipped to care; about yourself, and for those who need you. Carrying gratitude in your heart, joy as your wingwoman, and personal boundaries as your guardian angel.

And yes, this smacks of a privileged conversation; bear with me.

I'm a beginner in mid-life, now empowered to embody courage and excitement for my future. I made a pact to myself the day I flung myself off a cliff during my Grown Up's Gap Year trip – that if I survived that para jumping folly, I would take stock of what was truly necessary, enjoyable, and discard the rest.

The ending of all of this? I concluded the treasure you seek may well be inside yourself, the gem you've carried with you all along. Or perhaps not, so then you decide to make changes. Either way, you need to take the journey to understand this for yourself. And that, my darlings, is what we shall do – together.

Note to self: next time, check the travel insurance first.

When your focus is unearthing you (perhaps long forgotten), it's impossible to predict the outcome. As trite as it may sound, the key is to enjoy the journey and embrace the unknown.

So, this isn't a guidebook on how to ditch your life and jet off to a tropical island (though let's be honest, that's tempting). It's about rediscovering your spark, a value-led lifestyle, purpose and action at the forefront of daily decisions, feeling better – joyful seeking. A big hug for you in mid-life. And if that involves a temporary escape? Well, who am I to judge? Welcome to A Grown Up's Gap Year – an adventure you won't want to miss.

How to Use This Guidebook

I'll hazard you are probably tired – of so many things, including other people's 'great advice'. And maybe you've spent so long looking after everyone else that you've sacrificed your own wellbeing, and sense of self. As therapist Esther Perel suggests, 'Identity isn't a fixed state but a dynamic interplay between who we are and who others expect us to be.' Somewhere in the chaos, my identity had become entangled with everyone else's needs, and I was left wondering:

- What shape do I want for my life, now?

- When did I forget to take care of my wellbeing?

- What steps can I take to feel better?

- When did fun disappear?

- What do I value?

- Where is my creativity, for my life?

- How did everything get so complicated?

If you're nodding along, thinking 'Hell yes', this sounds like me, then welcome! You're in the right place.

I'm often asked, 'Why this book? Why you?'

Per usual, it started from 'little thought before big action'. As I moseyed around, I took to the modern-day version of 'the bush telegraph', sharing my journey on Instagram. Hesitant at first to speak of the elation at being thousands of kilometres away from husband and beloved offspring. Yet the euphoric sense of returning to self was undeniable. Publicly citing epiphanies on freedom runs the risk of coming across as self-indulgent, especially when many others remain firmly in the trenches of mothering or caregiving. Instead, many kind-hearted readers cheered me on, saying my tales gave them hope there remains a universe beyond. A place for you to rediscover what it is that gives your life shape and meaning.

Why me? Well, I have some professional chops to help you feel better, combined with a mind that constantly questions the status quo. More importantly, I've lived it – five decades on the front lines of a chequered life. You may find yourself in my story or in the stories of the wonderful women I share throughout this book. I have been at pains to:

- offer practical, handy hints for your busy life

- sift through the noise and avoid quackery

- remind you that this is not a dress rehearsal.

This guidebook shows you the journey upfront. None of this wading to the end to get the message gobbledygook. No esoteric mumbo jumbo where a few fragranced oils might pave the way to all seeing and knowing, no magic wand to absolve you of all your responsibilities. Neither is it chock-a-block with facts and figures. Other tomes do both of those well. I have written in soundbites because presumably you too have faces looking to you for everything, and little time to call your own. Getting to the nub of things succinctly – asking questions that swirled for me, then offering practical ideas for you to come to your answers, uncomplicate your life – and have a bloody good time doing it. That's it in a nutshell.

The way I approached reinvigorating, and the route I took, may not work for you. There is no one path, no one order; please dip in and out as curiosity takes you. If, from all angles, something looks good and has evidence to back it up, commit to giving it a go. The latest studies show the current stock of mid-lifers (us) might well exceed the 100-year mark. If (like me) you are in your fifties, that is an extraordinary amount of time to fill. Ageing in health and joy challenges you to:

- decide to take charge of your life and prioritise yourself

- streamline your lifestyle

- rediscover who you are and what shape you want for your life

- overcome obstacles that stand in the way of your aspirations (without sacrificing commitments and responsibilities)

- rediscover vitality

- seek joy and have fun

- run away, just for a while.

'But there is no way I can take time out, get away, and extract myself from my life,' squawks your inner naysayer. Hang in there – the catchy title not only promises something you desire. This book will deliver the steps needed for you to immerse yourself in each of what I've termed 'the four mid-life seasons':

WINTER   Feel Empowered
SPRING   Feel Reinvigorated
SUMMER   Feel Adventurous
AUTUMN   Feel Connected

The Seasons do not correspond with the calendar year as we know it – each season is a sense – you will know when you feel it.

I will use the term 'running away' – escape, flying the coop, head for the hills, scarper – but let us be clear. It is not intended to relieve you of everything in life that requires you. Instead, it is the idea that you will get to a place where you can find space, clear your head, and return to you. A refreshed, reinvigorated, fulfilled person who can live more fully, thrive – your life, your way. your next act. Commit to working through the journey. Remember, a 'Grown Up's Gap Year' is a term. No-one is suggesting you literally leave for a year. Although if you want, and can, go you. For most, it is more relatable to envisage setting aside 'a period of time for ourselves'. If that also involves a trip (which I highly recommend in whichever form that works for you), then super. I often thought about a desert island or a stint on Alone Australia in order to not be located. The solitude I would embrace … it's the bitey things that rival my fear of a hormonal teen. Thank you for showing up and entrusting me to guide you through your mid-life SEASONS; rediscover possibility, create space to call your own, seek joy, take inspired adventures, open your mind for positive choices – feel better. I will be extremely fulfilled if this guidebook inspires you to propel in curiosity. Take your version of a Grown Up's Gap Year.

TRY THIS

Sample as many of the 'try this' ideas as reasonable for your current circumstances.

- I suggest you buy a diary or notepad large enough to write your way through the practical exercises and anything else you wish to note down along the way.

THE JOURNEY
BEGINS

The Four Seasons of Mid-Life

Where Are We Heading on a Grown Up's Gap Year?

Joyful Seeking in the Four Seasons of Mid-Life sums things up quite neatly for our adventure. Encouraging you to get excited about what comes next – what shape you want your mid-life to take.

It's not a cliché to remind you to live your life with passion and purpose. It is never too late to chase down what you want or to begin anew. Our beliefs can limit us, but nothing arrives on our doorstep without effort.

If we are fulfilled, healthy, strong, engaged, happy, surrounded by community, looking out for others, resting, expanding, using food as medicine, spending time in nature, going on adventures, loving, exercising to invigorate, and presenting ourselves in vitality ... The world responds in kind. It just does.

Data shows mid-life women (in developed countries) are wealthier and more educated than ever. Our influence grows across economic, social, and cultural landscapes; remember this.

I've found making changes feels more manageable when I treat myself as a work in progress, like a PROJECT. Seeing myself from a place of abstract removes emotion and self-chatter. Putting steps in place with a fluid deadline alleviates pressure – there is no success or failure, no race to an imaginary finish line. Just the aim to keep moving forward. Repeat after me: *I am Project 'Fabulous Woman' (insert your name). I make my own mid-life life happen. I have a voice!*

In my experience, four mid-life stumbling blocks commonly arise:

1. **Discombobulation.** A sense of discomfort, dawning realisation that life is not a practice run – yet you can't quite put your finger on what may be missing.

2. **Wellbeing.** Nutrition, movement, sleep, and mindfulness. Feeling better.

3. **Clarity.** What we want, why we want it, and how to make lifestyle (and perhaps relationship) changes.

4. **Space.** Carving out time to get creative with possibilities.

Your mid-life and mine will arrive at different times, depending on our circumstances. This is why I'm not prescribing *A Grown Up's Gap Year* to a particular age – it's more a feeling than a date on the calendar. It's a time when you ask, 'What do I want for my foreseeable future?' If you struggle to answer, or the gap between your expected trajectory and your present circumstances feels vast, it may be time to step back.

Differing reasons, Different seasons

WINTER: Cocooning when I felt exhausted

SPRING: Emerging when I felt reinvigorated

SUMMER: Adventure-seeking when I felt expansive

AUTUMN: Reconnecting when I felt settled

Monique xx

Nuance of Each Season

Feel Empowered	Feel Reinvigorated	Feel Adventurous	Feel Connected
take stock	wellbeing	recharge	passion
dream	improve	freedom	review
seek	transformative	wild	peace
simplify	renew	attraction	joy
contemplate	focus	courageous	love
question	learn	solo	comfort
nurture	tenacity	immerse	settled
research	immerse	confidence	balance
reflect	practice	energise	lifestyle
prioritise	positive	travel	sustainable
process	ignite	bravery	authentic
insight	trust	experiment	genuine
organise	fearless	journal	harvest
design	resilience	explore	*ikigai*
creative	clarity	discover	community
disregard	belief	thrive	curate

Create Space in Your Four Seasons of Mid-Life

A Grown Up's Gap Year empowers you to create space for yourself.

Charts or acronyms do not work for me – I like to flow. But if you are bone-weary, you might want someone to say 'try this' – it bolstered me and might help you too.

I won't bombard you with self-help jargon; this isn't another book of fuzzy feelings and vague insights. Instead, I hope that by the last page, you'll have a plan of sorts in place, a notepad of practical steps – so you can start to take inspired action.

Using a loose analogy of the four seasons. Imagine your mid-life journey as passing through:

- WINTER   Feel Empowered (Taking stock, begin to plan)

- SPRING   Feel Reinvigorated (Renewal, focus on wellbeing)

- SUMMER   Feel Adventurous (Exploration, feel free)

- AUTUMN   Feel Connected (Consolidate, return, reflect)

Winter comes first, encouraging space to rest, recharge, and reflect – an essential pause before what's to come. Then, Spring ushers in fresh starts, curiosity, and a reinvigorated wellbeing roadmap. Summer brings with it energy, adventure, inspiration, and the boldness to step out of your comfort zone. Finally, Autumn invites you to gather the wisdom you've earned and consolidate your flow of transformation. All of this to allow you to evolve at your own pace, without rushing, making the process of rediscovery one that suits you and your timeframe.

Creating S.P.A.C.E. for yourself. I find providing a visual is helpful, to get a sense of where we are heading.

Simplify And Plan Your Future

I use this chart when facilitating retreats and thought you might find it handy too.

Finances, home, lifestyle. Clear external clutter to calm the mind.

Purpose, what is your reason to bounce out of bed in the morning?

Plan. Identify what brings value and joy, your dream future. Let go of what no longer serves you.

Why? External change can spark instant progress.

Action Your Wellbeing

Nutrition, movement, sleep, mindset. Align values with healthy behaviours.

Personal branding. Reflect on how you present yourself to the world.

Why? More energy to implement steps to age positively, and engage in vitality.

Connection

Curate meaningful relationships. Strengthen ties with friends, family, and community.
Professional and social contribution. Expand your influence and opportunities. Give back.

Why? Connection boosts happiness, health, and joy as we age.

Explore Novelty And Adventure

Travel, experiment, find joy. Seek new perspectives through travel, hobbies, and creative projects.
Freedom. Step outside your comfort zone to recalibrate and reconnect with yourself.

Why? New experiences keep you inspired and engaged with life.

A GROWN UP'S GAP YEAR IN A NUTSHELL

Overarching Theme

Give yourself a big hug, feel better, put you in the picture. Your life. Your way.

Throughout this book you will:

Learn to navigate four seasons of mid-life

Winter – Feel Empowered
Spring – Feel Reinvigorated
Summer – Feel Adventurous
Autumn – Feel Connected

Treat yourself as a design project S.P.A.C.E

Simplify Your Lifestyle
Plan With Purpose
Action Your Wellbeing
Connect with Your Later in Life Tribe
Explore Novelty and Adventure in mid-life

You Are Your 'Now' Project

Diary Note…

In the beginning, I needed to quell the horror amid the realisation there is no linear answer or path. The future will be what it will be. Along the way, I garnered that there are loads of us who fancy taking off into the sunset, yet this does not solve all. At some point, you need to face the music and take charge of your direction. Start somewhere; it doesn't matter where, although, if forced to pick a lane, feeling optimal in health and wellbeing is my best advice.

These things resonated with me (of course, yours may differ based on your values):

1. Wellbeing – the best physical and mental place I can create – health narrative, sleep, movement, nutrition – in that order. Ease flows from this point.

2. Having a champion – someone who calls bullshit, builds you up, listens, helps on the home front if you are not there – a coach, a sister, a mother, a friend. You'll know who the right ones are in your life.

3. Sorting your 'things' before you pack your suitcase. Emotional and physical baggage can be weighty if left unattended.

My Grown Up's Gap Year was one of utter introspection, navel-gazing, line in the sand, looking back, looking forward, wavering, pondering. Frankly exhausting me and anyone generous enough to follow along (cheering from the sidelines, showing kindness and care) – it is my wish you also find such generosity. But sometimes a firmer plan is necessary, especially during periods of uncertainty. Chapters of practical, handy hints follow – from a place of 'been there, done that'. Yet I believe you may not feel like starting without an initial boost – first run on the board as it were. The dopamine hit when you just want shhh and a lie-down but know you will benefit from sparking your energy. Sometimes, simply feeling better is all it takes. I invite you to follow the suggestions throughout the next few pages and let's see where the rest takes you.

Begin Here Tomorrow Morning

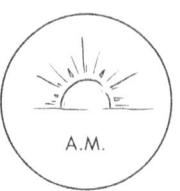

Life is busy; sometimes all too hard. What can make it more palatable is to quell the inane chatter we sometimes loop over and over. Frankly, the mind games are more exhausting than the actual doing. Begin to replace any noise of 'I should have …' with 'I have ….'

The Zen Buddhist word *zengosaidan* encapsulates this brilliantly:

Don't put off 'fill in the blank' until tomorrow, or your thoughts will be distracted by the as yet undone.

I encourage you to try the following as an experiment – a morning practice to set you up for a positive day. At the very least, whatever unfolds, you had a moment of brightness and a sense of completion. Research shows it is a simple yet beneficial way to begin living a life of joyful seeking!

I do better 'getting done' early – you may prefer otherwise. Just give yourself two weeks to see if my method works.

Kind Start

I call my morning practice 'Kind Start' – because there is a good chance if you begin the day with kindness to yourself, you're more likely to establish a solid foundation for whatever life throws your way. When my eyes open, I switch to autopilot, diving into a routine so ingrained I 'do' rather than 'think'. It's my anchor. This regime isn't ticking boxes; it's consistently following what works to nurture my wellbeing. Like Spanx for your day, it holds everything together. It's freeing, not restrictive – adapt as necessary. Enjoy starting your day in kindness for you, so you can keep showing up for everyone else.

 Wake Up At The Same Time

 Make Bed

 Brisk Short Walk Facing The Sun

 Cold Blast Shower

If I miss my usual exercise, I still make time to get outside – perhaps a ten-minute walk then add movement 'snacks' in the day.

 15 Minutes Getting Your Home In Order

 Pack Your Pre-Prepared Lunch (done the night before, more to follow on nutrition, for now have a decent 'real food' lunch and avoid excess snacking and ultra-processed foods)

Each of these ideas is underpinned by a certified study – helping to reap a myriad of benefits. See my website.

Oh, and whilst it is not on the list because I was not doing this while I had the morning family rush, I now light an incense stick. Subliminally, the scent works to imbibe a sense of 'I can', an intention to self. If you are still in the trenches of a frantic morning with all eyes on you, know I know, you are vibing telling me where to shove my sweet-smelling idea.

SIDENOTE – Lymphatic Drainage Dry brush or exfoliate pre-shower; it invigorates and sloughs away dead skin cells and may also assist with stimulating lymphatic drainage. I combine this with contrast hot/cold therapy which we will read about soon.

Do your research before you decide it is for you, and to understand the correct method.

Ideas To Get You Going

Getting in the habit of 'writing things out' is incredibly cathartic – grab a notebook and start jotting notes on the following questions (take small action steps):

TRY THIS

Exercises are best handwritten. Studies show writing improves memory, retention of new info, and habit formation. Seeing words on paper helps cement them – no hiding in online files.

1. **Identify five areas in your life – physical or emotional – that are overdue for a good clear-out.** Write these down and create one action step for each. Contemplate; begin.

Find a list of health checks you can take to your doctor in the chapter 'No-One Knows Your Body Better Than You'.

2. **Where do you feel most alive?** What activities, places, or people make you feel like your truest self?

3. **Check in with your body – schedule a baseline health check.** Gain control of your personal health narrative.

4. **Plan a solo day trip, even to the next suburb.** Discover the joy of your own company.

5. **Start a daily walking practice.** Whether it's a brisk 10-minute walk or a longer stroll, this activity will boost your physical and mental health.

6. **Practise saying 'Why not?' to new experiences.** Try one fresh *yes* every day for a week.

7. **Tackle one small decluttering project in your home.** Maybe it's that drawer that seems to breed old receipts and stray pens – suddenly you'll find room for fresh ideas and possibility.

Quote from author Anne Lamott's husband – 'Everything true and beautiful can be seen or experienced on a 10-minute walk if you're paying attention.'

By mid-life, we are layers of our lifetime. Broken parts, buried incidents, joyous times.

Only you will know your story.

These threads bind us, humanity in all its beauty and blemishes.

The Japanese art and philosophy of kintsugi encapsulates the sentiment: mending broken pottery with gold, where every crack becomes part of a new, stronger design. Instead of hiding the flaws,

it celebrates them.

Embrace all your parts – celebrate you.

Monique xx

How Did We Get Here?

Dear Gen X,

This moment of introspection – a foreign state for our collective. Possibly, until recently, you've had a fairly firm handle on your place in the world. Born in the '60s and '70s to parents so young they were barely formed themselves – sorting nappies and sleepless nights in their early twenties. In my twenties, I was sorting weekends away and late nights out partying. Oh, my parents partied, they just did it with their kids in tow. We learned quickly to sleep  anywhere – the back of a Kingswood cheek-to-jowl with the cousins, or under a table at the neighbours. Mum and Dad worked hard to save for what they needed then went shopping. In our twenties, we went shopping then worked stupid hours to pay back what we owed and more (with interest).

Childhood family holidays probably involved a caravan, lots of relatives, sunburn, and not an adult in sight until the BBQ was lit at sunset. If you came from a fancy family, you might have swung a tropical holiday to Club Med. FOMO didn't exist because, by the time you found out you weren't invited, the event had already been and gone (one phone line meant plenty of calls were missed). As for 'stuff', there wasn't much. Some had Myer accounts or Country Road clothes – the rest of us had part-time jobs at Katies or McDonald's and made do with putting a Wham

T-shirt on layby. A weekly thrill was the local record shop where we collected the (free) top 40 songs list, later crowding around the only family TV to watch bands on *Countdown*. Oh, and Sundays were 'shut up shop' time, devoted to family lunches and picnics (or annoyingly vigorous hikes if my 'over' active parents had anything to do with it). Either way, there was a day of little expectation beyond recharging batteries.

By the time we left uni, TAFE, teachers college, nursing school, air hostess training or finished a trade, cheap airfares were in full swing. The starter trip (Contiki Europe, booze-fuelled) was followed by Bali or Thailand, maybe India. With our cultural horizons widened, we were either having too much fun to get hitched or desperately seeking it in all the wrong places. *Seinfeld* hit the screens, *Melrose Place, 90210, Friends,* later *Sex and the City* – they navigated life for us and let us know it was okay to do 'it' differently from our parents.

Coined the 'latchkey kids', we were the ones who simply got on with what it was we were meant to be getting on with. No-one (read parents in the '70s) asked what we wanted; we didn't necessarily ask that of ourselves. At some point, we set a course and moved along 'that' path. You can't pigeonhole an entire generation – of course, some of us found success and others floundered – generally what we started is pretty much how it remained. Career of sorts, married probably, kids perhaps, divorce a good chance, widowed sadly for some.

If we went the kids route, we started 'parenting'. An all-consuming, expensive, full-time job to go with our other full-time jobs. If you were in a career, Gordon Gecko told you 'greed is good', so you worked harder to buy more, take the kids on extraordinary 'educational' holidays – basically they came everywhere we had wanted to go but no-one took us. Suddenly, there wasn't so much time for extended family – cousins were once a year. Grandparents were still very much on the scene, more hands-on than they had been for their kids (us). Having it all costs money, childcare is expensive, and someone needed to sort the 'activities' – pick up/drop offs, the class birthday parties, the language lessons, music lessons, the specialist doctors' appointments, the carefully curated 'healthy' dinners, the nutritionists, psychologists, the school events (requiring parental attendance).

Keeping this show on the road took energy.

Our Gen Z young adults – there is a good chance they still hover around the nest. Our career? Either in tatters due to being 'parent on deck' for the most part, or simply no longer fitting us. Parents, getting on a bit, we can see what is coming – we want to help them, will help them – but currently we are sad, mad, and tired. Somewhere amongst 'having it all', we lost ourselves.

No surprise then that, quite recently, I didn't recognise my world anymore. I could not envisage future possibilities. In observing friends from all walks of life, I realised this was a 'middle class mid-life malaise'. Curiosity and creativity lost somewhere. As I finally asked, 'What do I want?' – the greatest irony, I had no bloody idea. I'm missing in action from my own life. Help.

Love and Good Luck

with A Grown Up's Gap Year xx

PS If I forget to mention it later, given all this, it's no wonder we are pooped. Make sure you cut yourself some slack.

First, a Few Things to Get Off Our Chest

This is not a guidebook on parenting. However, as I am 'Mum', it is through this lens that much will follow. Insert your situation. The thread is 'caring' – about loved ones, friends, work, community, life, the world – all the things directly in your orbit, including what you have a relationship with but zero control over.

The Joyful Art of Giving Might Well Become Joyless (*if it threatens loss of self*).

When Your Tank is Full of 'Everything' – Mental Load, the Last Frontier

When you're doing such a great job of being a mum or 'carer', it's easy to forget where you fit in the world.

As mums, it is our role to keep our babies safe and secure physically and emotionally. But as women, we do this *and* 'the rest'. The bone-deep exhaustion of sleepless nights, the heart-pounding panic of near-misses, school lunches, doctors' appointments, work deadlines, gift-buying – the minutiae of managing everything can leave us spent. The emotional and intellectual labour we shoulder for everyone else has us depleted before the day even begins.

In *On Our Best Behaviour*, author Elise Loehnen explores how women internalise caregiving as a societal duty, often running on empty before we realise it. Over time, caregiving morphs into expectation, draining us without our awareness.

Mothers bring divergent backgrounds, personalities, circumstances. We do the best with what we have. The mental load we carry every day is the constant hum no-one else seems to notice.

A Grown Up's Gap Year Diary note...

The minute I open my eyes on the first day of my 'geographically farthest from home' Gap moment, my phone trills. One of my 'man-children', sobbing. Heart-wrenching moment for them, otherwise earth-shattering – no. Sad, but safe. I listen a moment. My heart breaks for them, but something shifts. 'Perhaps call your father,' I weakly offer. 'I have to go, darling.'

No longer the only 24/7 problem-solver. Now, my calendar includes non-negotiable 'me time', and I've retired from my unpaid role as Chief Domestic Officer. It's about balancing being there for my loved ones while also nurturing myself – after all, you can't pour from an empty cup, can you?

This is where the Festival of Me begins. I will return to my loves 'more and less' – more centred, less restless.

As we reclaim space for ourselves, the mental load may feel heavier at first, but it's crucial to set boundaries and delegate where we can.

Parenting as a Verb: The Hand We Have Played in Messing Up Our Kids

Parenting as a verb – a constant, relentless activity that somehow defined an entire generation of well-meaning parents. I naively thought preschool was for play, social interaction – not ensuring they could read the newspaper before age five. But that was just the tip of the iceberg; lurking beneath the surface a clear message I had to up my game. I'll never forget when, hosting a child's birthday party, I was informed I should have provided every guest with a prize during *pass the parcel* – apparently, everyone had to win! Or the time a mother called me in distress, wondering why our sons weren't best friends despite her efforts to orchestrate their every interaction. These little moments, while seemingly harmless, add up to a culture where we prevent our children from experiencing even the smallest disappointments. It's the over-scheduling, too – piling on extracurriculars until there's no time for them to *contemplate their navels*.

Somewhere along the way, societal aspirations skyrocketed. Helicopter parenting wasn't something I set out to do, but it became inevitable in a world where being 'just a good parent' was no longer enough. The 1990s marked the beginning of this seismic shift in parenting culture, reaching its full stride by the 2000s. We evolved from being parents (the noun) to actively parenting (the verb) – scheduling, monitoring, protecting, orchestrating every moment of our children's lives.

You may recall I've acknowledged my 'sticky digits' in my patch – so no emails calling me out for not 'stepping out of this race' – my observations, not pointing fingers.

As I concluded writing this book, Dr Danielle Einstein and Dr Judith Locke released theirs, speaking directly to my conundrum

53

in their book *Raising Anxiety*. They argue that overprotective, interventionist parenting – the type that cushions every potential fall – has contributed to a generation who struggle with resilience. Einstein's work highlights that when we remove all uncertainty, we send the message that uncertainty is to be feared.

The result? From my 'vox pop' conversations with other parents, the kids want out – they want to be independent – but the financial reality means staying at home is a necessity. However, another layer exists here; does it also stem from this parental-induced anxiety? Have we – through hovering and over-scheduling – left them less capable of managing life's complexities?

While the reasons are multifaceted, here we are – ready to reclaim some space for ourselves without the guilt. Because, as it turns out, being less available might actually be good for everyone. A dawning of the need to step back and rediscover ourselves after decades of hyper-vigilance. A Grown Up's Gap Year.

Studies show that between 1981 and 2021, the time parents spent actively engaging with their children more than doubled, while children's independence significantly decreased.

Prioritising You

Without exception. All the women I interviewed proceeded to tell me how busy life is, tending to all that is required of them. They explained first how they love their (insert: person/people/pets) – and without doubt they (and I) do.

I asked permission to acknowledge this important fact then pop it to one side.

I deeply understand.

Compounded by working from 'home' for the best part of a couple of decades. Continually attempting to catch time meant I often willed away the 'precious moments' in-between. Of course, there were times to lie under a tree and gaze at the wonder of clouds with my babies – but for the most part, I confess to having one constant eye on the horizon. This is incredibly detrimental to finding peace within.

Not one woman prefaced our chat with how much they prioritise themselves first.

Prioritising yourself, even if you remain as 'adjudicator for all', allows you to change the narrative. Being purposeful, creative, and curious about your wellbeing takes time, energy, and inclination. I suspect you have the latter because you are here. Energy and time are another matter altogether.

Years of a low-grade simmering fury at 'my boundaries' being ignored whilst my husband was an A Grader at sticking his needs front line and centre. Perhaps he has it right – the balance between caring enough and self-preservation.

It took running away to be able to reframe freedom. I now understand this state to be putting a fence around what I need – an impending project (or feeling overwhelmed) I now physically remove myself for pockets of time in order to reclaim expanse and sanity for me and those close to me.

So, I Suspect You Need More Time For You

Now you've started to flick through the book, your heart might be sinking. Why?

You read the contents and realised to go from:

• Stuck, Uninspired, Pooped
To:
• Inspired, Heart Full Of Possibility, Energised

requires you to pay attention, write, think, find room in a packed life.

'I don't have any spare time,' you cry.

You probably don't because you are a normal person with the ton of responsibilities we've acknowledged. The treadmill of modern existence keeps our poor legs perpetually running to keep up with a life that doesn't ever allow us to catch a breath, except, amidst all that responsibility, you are going to commit to locating a moment or two you CAN claw back for yourself.

A Reflection on Personal Responsibility

Joan Didion captured the essence of this journey when she wrote: *'Character – the willingness to accept responsibility for one's own life – is the source from which self-respect springs.'* This struck a chord. Should you still be waiting for life to happen, mid-life is the point at which we stop and take ownership of where we place our time

The 'fit your oxygen mask first' premise.

and energy. The flow-on of 'making some time, your own time' will be for loved ones.

TRY THIS

Take an audit of everything you are needing to continue to do. It is an important list, but we are moving swiftly because obligation can weigh heavily on gaining traction.

1. What can be outsourced? 2. Where are you wasting time – mindless TV, endless scrolling on social media?

If you can recoup 15 minutes each day, this equates to almost 2 hours per week to spend improving your lot. Double this and you get four hours. Commit five days to trial this exercise. Take notes on your progress, tweak as you need, keep the momentum!

Now put a 15-minute block in your diary every day, just for you. 100% focus. Lie on the grass, read, walk – anything, as long as it's about you. No phone, no calls, no sharing. Announce to your posse you're on 'Do Not Disturb'. I find morning best – set the alarm 15 minutes earlier, sit still with a coffee, or take a brisk walk. It's my version of meditation. Just 15 minutes can help refocus on what will serve you best in your lifestyle.

If you have opened up this book with the lure of procuring a few new wellbeing tips, maybe a sideline of travel ideas – suddenly you find yourself reading about thrusting yourself off cliffs and into the unknown.

Seeking greener pastures, hunting down your why.

When, thank you very much, the view from where you reside is absolutely fine and you have zero interest in scaling any mountains to get to 'another place'.

Brilliant. Own your patch and your comfort zone.

Skip on to the chapters that call to you or pass on the book to another friend who may be faltering.

Monique xx

Begin at the End, Then Add Yes

Tell me, what is it you plan to do with your one wild and precious life?

– Mary Oliver

A Grown Up's Gap Year Diary Note …

I'm about to jump off a cliff with instructions that amount to not much more than:

'Run with straight legs … then run as normal … then you will be up and away,' my instructor Linus says with a grin.

'Like waterskiing,' I clarify. 'The straight legs?'

Except, as Linus yells 'run', I remember waterskiing is straight arms, not legs – and as I am the front runner, I wonder for a split second if it is possible for me to f**k this up, although that might have been a question for earlier – not as the cliff is nigh.

I cannot understand why, as I run stiffly towards the edge, I am not panicking. A soupçon of adrenaline, yes. Panic, no. Then a slight tug, a whisper of upward pull – and we are flying. Whooshing air as we ascend, and then peace as we bob along with the updraft. Terrifying! We drift toward a peak – thick with tall, summer green pine trees which grow infinitely shorter as we soar skyward. Briefly, I muse if I will end up impaled on the timber fence way below – but then, release, as I morph into someone I used to be. Spur of the moment. Ever-trusting. Fun. Lighter somehow.

I survive my para jump. Back on terra firma, I continue to float, exhilarated for several hours. Later, after hurtling some thousands of metres at great speed strapped to a – well, strapping young Austrian gent – there were two reactions from those who know me:

Later, you will read the story of Mr Eddie Jaku to underline this point.

friends made since I have been a mum said, 'It was completely out of character'; family and older friends laughed and said, 'That sounds about right.' They were both correct.

And I am thrilled to discover I can still have a foot in both camps – show up for 'hell yes' at the drop of a hat and know when 'no' suits the situation better. A balanced approach to joyful seeking.

Deciding to Be Joyful

How to strike the balance? The purposeful art of deciding to be joyful. Note the subtle nuance – this is not seeking joy – as if joy is a state to be found once and remain forever more in your grasp.

No, everything that comes next is intended to be an exploration of hope, possibilities, creativity, wellbeing. Choosing a demeanour of joyful as your companion while you go looking – well that will be the golden ticket to perhaps finding precisely what you need.

Understand that achieving a constant joyful state is unrealistic. For you, now might be about survival – keeping a business afloat and a family healthy and 'together'. Yet dreams and plans are free; they keep hope and spirits alive. History shows that those who find themselves in untenable situations yet spare a thought to possibility – a reminder that joy exists – thrive.

Life should not be a journey to the grave with the intention of arriving safely in a pretty and well-preserved body, but rather to skid in broadside in a cloud of smoke, thoroughly used up, totally worn out, and loudly proclaiming 'Wow! What a ride!'

– Hunter S Thompson

When I 'ran away', it was to reclaim a sense of adventure. The reward? Even the 'mundane' felt new and exciting – something as basic as not knowing the aisles of the supermarket off by heart was weirdly thrilling. Adulting forces you to have linear days as well as routine, and because of 'life admin', we often forget to be playful and have fun. Wouldn't it be a shame to get to the end of it all and feel like that sweet sense of novelty passed you by? Learning to say hell yes or why not again, rather than overanalysing all the 'why I should nots' is liberating.

Your Time Is Now

Mid-life is the point where there is nowhere left to hide. You also hold the added gift of hindsight. Many researchers and books examine top laments of the dying, generally falling into:

- not chasing what may have made them happy
- not spending more quality time with beloved friends and family
- not getting work/life balance more balanced
- not focusing on wellbeing (physical, mental) in order to spend longer 'in health'

• not living a life of self-belief and courage.

Four significant deaths propelled my 'gap year' – my oldest friend (his passing set me on a reawakening), a beloved pet a few weeks later. Mid-trip, Olivia Newton John died. The impetus for my 'just do it' para jumping escapade.

Later that month in London, the Queen signalled out.

With this, I decided it was time to rein things in and headed home.

Fully grasping our time is finite has a way of galvanising. Rather than a 'full stop', I see freedom – to stop looking for validation, make the plans, take the opportunity to pursue passions and dreams, to just 'do', loosen controlling tendencies, flow. Initially, I became a tad manic in my pursuit of making every moment count – carefree – and if I am entirely honest, a little careless, too.

It was delightful to meet the younger version of me again, for a while. All well and good, except life cannot be sustained through a hedonistic, teenage-phase, myopic lens. Not in my world – most likely not in yours, either. As I segued from overthinking every aspect of life to giving many things little thought, I settled that my future self would weigh up options and say yes more often, as it works for my present state of affairs. Joyful seeking with my mantra: '**Why not now?**'

What I Wish Someone Had Told Me

(Possibly my parents did, though God knows I didn't listen)

We All Wobble

Understand this. no-one knows what they are doing 100% in life, not a single human. If they say they do, I say 'Pinocchio'. We may be able to go through our paces in our 'arena', have practical knowledge, a natural inclination, be able to bumble our way through. But 100% certainty – not a chance.

'Impostor syndrome' is the jazzed-up term. I prefer 'I just don't want to look like a twit'. It is not a syndrome, it is a state – one you can push through with a bit of effort, chutzpah, and some tricks up your sleeve.

You don't have to know everything – remember this and life becomes less daunting.

When my boys were young, and the new school year drew close, a rumble of uncertainty began for what lay ahead. Who would be their teacher, would they have the same friends, what if …? As parents, we want to smooth their crinkled little brow and lie. 'Everything will always be fine,' we tell them. However, it won't, not always. Instead, I would write them a card imparting a piece of wisdom they could file away in the 'my mum is crazy' drawer. I persisted, every year. If just one of my 'pearls' came in handy, my job was done. I am sure my parents did the same and, of course, I took no notice … so I wrote a retrospective letter to myself.

Dear Wide-Eyed Young Me,

Set your course early, but don't be afraid to take a scenic detour or two.

1. *You don't need to have your entire life mapped out – just have an idea of what makes you feel good, what interests you. That way, if you are blown off the path along the way – financial setbacks; ill health – you can still look to the end game. Without it, you'll be drifting like a cork in the ocean of life – and trust me, that ocean gets choppier as the years fly by.*

2. *Passion is great, but it's not the holy grail of existence. If you can't find it, don't sweat it. Joy in the everyday is the real secret.*

3. *Trust your gut. About people and situations. Don't stay somewhere you are unhappy. Rarely – if ever – will things improve.*

4. *Money can make you comfortable and afford you choice. It can give you the ability to be generous. Have fun with it; don't squander it; plan for the future. But don't worship it (unless it buys you a ticket somewhere sunny)! Love it for what you can do with it – not what it can do for you.*

5. *If people piss you off, give them an inch – they might be having a bad day. Offer to help. If they continue to piss you off – do not be afraid to tell them. Be mindful a wolf can appear in sheep's clothing. Don't ever be a doormat because you feel you do not have a voice. Practise roaring sometimes; it feels good.*

6. *In victory, be humble-ish. In defeat, be gracious. But always let them know you're a force to be reckoned with.*

7. *Manners (and courtesy) are never out of fashion; they will take you a long way. In fact, the whole way.*

8. *Above all, you are just as good as anyone else. Never let anyone's title or status make you feel inferior. People are people – we all wake up, go to the loo, have a shower, get dressed, and start our days.*

9. *Have a bloody good time and smile. A heartfelt smile can take you the whole way.*

Love, Your Slightly Older, Marginally Wiser Self

TRY THIS

Write your own letter and tuck it away for when you need a reminder that you've come this far. And in the meantime, don't sweat the small stuff!

Or print this one.

Read this wonderful little book: *Don't Sweat the Small Stuff … and It's All Small Stuff* – a '90s bestseller by Richard Carlson.

There are undertakings that have long sat on my list of 'things to accomplish in this lifetime' that may remain unfulfilled when I drop off my perch.

Far from regret, instead a spring in my step without the weight of expectation and self-imposed longing that might have served me better to dispel decades ago.

I'm all for chasing dreams, but being too future-focused can let the present slip away.

Monique xx

Listening to Wisdom

Chatting to my fit and engaged 83-year-old Papa, I asked for his wellbeing mantra – I received the following note:

Dear Eldest Daughter,

Not everything in my life has gone according to plan, but what I do know is a guardrail of sorts helps me feel consistently joyful – even when the road gets bumpy.

Key factors contributing to a joyful demeanour

- *Living with a trusted life partner and experiencing love*
- *Regular communication with family*
- *A small circle of true friends*
- *Active outdoors lifestyle, daily yoga, and meditation practice*
- *Healthy eating habits*
- *Understanding that nothing is more certain than change*
- *Lifelong learning, awareness of current and global affairs*
- *Love of reading*
- *Social and community contacts, projects, and supporting selected charities*
- *Passion for ethical, moral, and sustainable values*
- *Love of nature and the planet*
- *Practising a creative hobby, writing, gardening*

Isn't this beautiful? Perfect, actually.

Understand This

Dad's list has served him through the ups and downs. Should life feel burdensome to navigate, a guide is especially important when creativity for how to reclaim joy may seem light on the ground. So, what to do? Acknowledge a few-truths:

- Accept there is no magic 'right way' or 'wrong way' to do life.

- 'All at once' is NOT a sustainable state.

- Are you scared? Welcome to the club. Rest assured none of us have skipped this path before – we are in this together. Now that's more comforting to know, isn't it?

- Learn the art of the ASK.

Asking for help is hard – as women it is often confronting – as we are conditioned to be givers. Contemplate for a moment, what is the worst that can happen if someone says no? Then what? As a real estate professional, my mum learned to see no as a question. Don't back away; instead, communicate what it is you need and ask for what you want. If you don't express this, no-one will know how to help.

Hers was a successful 35-year career in a cutthroat profession; we should take note.

If you don't know, chapters follow to help rediscover your WHY.

- Reflect on what key factors contribute to your wellbeing and happiness.

Wisdom surrounds us.

TRY THIS

I love chatting to wise folk. They seem to have their life together, floundering days behind them. Go and have a cup of tea with someone over 75 years old and ask what is important to them, what they wish they hadn't bothered with, and those things they wish they had not put off until later. Their wellbeing mantra.

There's much to learn from a straightforward approach to life.

I'd love it if you approach everything with an open mind. Many women I speak with have a shopping list of WHAT they want. As we strip away the guff, what is revealed is a deep loss of self. This realisation can be energising. Use it to your advantage to light the proverbial fire to get you moving!!

Monique xx

WINTER
FEEL EMPOWERED

Time to take stock – to know where you are now.

Practically speaking, Winter is the season to:

1. Start reinvigorating your well being routine.

    2. Declutter your environment.

      3. Sort your financial literacy.

        4. Identify your values.

Be the Star of Your Show, Rolling Up Your Sleeves for Project You

Above all, be the heroine of your life, not the victim.

– Nora Ephron

We are all at different life stages – kids or not, partner, solo, maybe ageing parents, work, finances. Apply ideas that are realistically appropriate to your lifestyle and state of affairs. Return to others later. I wasn't 'running away' when my kids were at school. I won't 'run away' when and if my parents require care. My direction was right for the time. The stories women have contributed to this book vary in order to reflect a patchwork of life experiences.

Depleted humans are not created the same; some of us work out but eat junk; others keep impeccable homes but feel emotionally cluttered. We could all benefit from a 'do-over' – starting with our health narrative and then our 'chic' (how we present ourselves to the world).

I can never decide whether it is better to:

- guide a 'discovery' of values

- tackle your health first

- clarify your financial situation

- jump in the car (plane, boat, bicycle, shanks pony) and take off to clear your head.

What resonates?

- If you feel healthy, then rolling up your sleeves to 'design' your next part seems more doable.

- Dragging yourself out of bed on a cold and wet early morning to exercise might be easier if you have a vision for your 'why'.

- If you are entangled beyond all reason, sometimes 'time out' to retreat within is required – simply to breathe so the rest can flow.

- If you have put financial literacy in the too-hard basket or handed the reins to someone else – then empowering yourself with knowledge and options will provide strength (and reduce stress).

Taking Centre Stage

Remember sage sister Michelle's words: *'Untethered you is a dangerous state.'*

When I finally concluded that mid-life is simply another beginning, limited only by lack of curiosity, the runway became clearer. Your limits will only be things you decide you don't enjoy or require more effort than you can be bothered.

Life is not an unattainable, rainbow-filled, unicorn-strewn paradise – a candy-coloured ship will not sail you across the horizon to an existence lived in calm waters. This is reality, not fairyland. Instead, plan to adopt the following uncomplicated process – practical action steps that you can try right now.

As we discussed in the Four Mid-Life Seasons framework, you'll know when it's time to cocoon or adventure – it's all about feeling your way through your seasons.

Rolling Up Your Sleeves

At the onset of my 'Gap Moment', I stood on the sidelines of my life. I've now taken centre stage. It is there for you too! Be the star of your own show and embrace project you.

My dream is to inspire you to propel in curiosity for your journey.

Confused about where to begin? Read on …

Your Mid-Life Journey Quiz

My home environment is ...?
A. Lickety-split and organised.
B. Cupboards are for hiding the clutter, aren't they?
C. Organised I am, yet I have so much it takes a long time to stay this way.

Who are you responsible for?
A. I have an empty nest.
B. I have school-aged children.
C. I care for aging family/friends.

It's time to eat. What do you do?
A. I have no idea what to eat.
B. I have a nutritious plan for my meals.
C. I know what healthy food looks like, I just don't eat it.

How many days do you exercise each week?
A. Rarely or never.
B. 4 or more days.
C. 1–3 days.

When was the last time you took time out for yourself, alone?
A. I can't remember.
B. Within the last week.
C. Within the last month.

Do you know what is most important to you in your life?
A. Not really sure.
B. Yes, I am very clear about it.
C. I have an idea but often forget to prioritise it.

Do you bounce out of bed in the morning with a purpose in mind?
A. Rarely or never.
B. Yes, almost every day.
C. Sometimes, but not consistently.

Are you too exhausted to know where to start with planning a Grown Up's Gap Year?
A. Completely overwhelmed.
B. Not at all, I'm ready to plan.
C. A bit tired but could manage some planning.

Your favourite self-help read is?
A. I don't read self-help books.
B. A book that offers practical life advice.
C. An inspirational biography or story.

Have you been consistent with your health checks?
A. I rarely go for health checks.
B. Yes, I regularly keep up with them.
C. I go occasionally, but not as often as I should.

Do you know exactly what you are capable of?
A. Not really. I often doubt myself.
B. Yes, I am confident in my abilities.
C. I have some idea, but don't always utilise my full potential.

Results:

- Mostly As: Start with exploring – Summer – It might be time for new horizons. Discover more about yourself through travel or different opportunities.

- Mostly Bs: Start with streamlining – Winter – What You value. What really matters to you.

- Mostly Cs: Start with reinvigorating – Spring – Become a wellbeing whiz. Focusing on your health and wellbeing could be the key to improving your overall quality of life.

Invisible? Irrelevant? Absolutely Not!

You don't have to be fearless. Just don't let fear stop you. Live your life as though your real self is right there in every moment.

– Cheryl Strayed

It gets on my goat when we are still portrayed as silver and sedate (in the media and by brands) – these images do not speak for me. I am hopeful the twinset of invisibility and irrelevance foist upon our grandmothers and mothers once 'past a certain age' is, for the most part, not going to be our lot.

It behoves us to remain engaged, to be contributing community members. That's it really, isn't it? A sense of belonging, our tribe. Where you fit in the world. When that position shifts, that is when we can lose imagination for our life.

I need not repeat the cliche 'life is not a dress rehearsal', but my mum suggested it is worth repeating: 'Life is not a dress rehearsal'.

Invisibility in mid-life might become a cloak some unwittingly don. There is truth in feeling 'less fresh, sparkly, frontline, and centre' – a twinge of feeling passed over. One minute you're contributing, the next it's shades of standing on the sidelines at school sports day, last to be assigned to a team.

Society can only move so fast; the collective is a large beast to manoeuvre. I encourage you to show the world how you intend to age. Let them catch up to you. My friends and I don't find each other diminished, my family find my 'vigour' exhausting, and I'm fitter than I've been in decades. I've also learned the wonderful gift of age: you stop giving a toot about what others think.

Know this: you have a choice.

If your moment in the sun has taken a backseat while you nurtured others – kids, parents, partners – take a moment to acknowledge that work and pat yourself on the back. But now it's time to re-enter your own story. I don't have all the answers. I also cannot FIX you. Sharing what worked for me when I slumped through each day uncertain of my future is the best I can offer. The rest, my friends, is up to you. Let's agree to draw a line in the sand – from this line on, you will put your best foot forward to keep your eyes and ears open for opportunities.

Irrelevant? Invisible? Absolutely not.

Find Your Armour Every Day

My mum, Cornelia, always says, 'Never leave the house without your 'version' of armour.' Her 'version' is lipstick – which is not simply about appearance – but mindset. A way of showing up for the world, no matter what. Develop your own ritual. Even small shifts can create momentum. I found that switching out of gym gear during

my career reboot reframed my mindset. It would have been easy to stay in 'activewear', but changing into 'work mode' clothes gave me confidence – even when my office was just my walk-in wardrobe.

Tell me you have watched the viral activewear YouTube video; ha ha – that was me!

Micro-confidence – start working your confidence muscle every day and the process becomes easier. Forget 'fake it 'til you make it' – there's nothing fake about this. It's practising confidence by acting as if you're already there. Don't wait for the 'perfect' moment. Start.

Author Anne Lamott says, 'Perfectionism will keep you cramped and insane your whole life.'

TRY THIS

1. One small action toward. 'If I was already living as if ...'. Commit to it, daily.

2. Role models. Think of someone who inspires you – who embodies the traits you admire. Borrow from their playbook.

The Exhilaration of Embracing Possibility

Diary Note mid A Grown Up's Gap Year...

A late-night conversation with 'middle sister' reminds me that, back in the day, I used to live hard and joyfully. I was extremely resourceful, brave, adventurous, my world expansive. I'd move to new places alone, take on jobs that stretched me. I loved being outside; I'd bungee-jump, run marathons, swim in deep oceans, complete triathlons, ski black runs, drive deserted highways, apply for professional roles that were a massive stretch ... then life became busier, and I grew softer, lost my edge. I started to live passively, rather than actively.

And what a waste of the gift of life.

Granted, with responsibility there is less on 'your' terms and more compromise – that is adulting and gladly so.

Now, I don't need to move mountains, just be sure to actually live – stretch into possibilities rather than dwell in lack.

Just Start Doing

In mid-life, the world can be your oyster. With age comes freedom, a sudden realisation that you might as well 'just do it' – travel, go back and study, live in a new location, indulge your passion – please yourself after pleasing others for decades. Don't let past missteps or rejections prevent you from chasing down what you want in your life. Make this commitment to yourself:

I Will

- keep an open mind
- understand no-one else can do the work for me
- maintain momentum so I propel through increments (baby steps)
- be really clear there is no right way or wrong way
- remember everything is on the table – I am experimenting, and I am taking my time to find my way
- know, this time tomorrow, next week, next month, next year, next decade – I will feel incredibly empowered for taking action
- promise if I stumble one day, the next I will be back up and at it
- Choose curious – the sibling of boldness
- align values with the shape I want for my life.

Let us be clear, it is never too late. When I was 21 and at law school, there was a woman in my lectures who was 50 years old – ancient, I thought at the time. I now appreciate she would have graduated in her mid-fifties with at least 20 years working in her 'new' career. A four-year degree seemed like forever to me – to this woman, it would have been 'two ticks' in the scheme of things.

I feel we owe it to our grandmas and mums who didn't have the opportunity for these conversations. Conversely, our daughters and sons are watching – as they begin to take independent steps into the world.

Why not now?

Melinda Louise Hutchings is a valued member of my 'later in life' tribe. Her story is a powerful reminder that while the outcome of changing lanes is never guaranteed, one thing is clear: you'll never know what's possible unless you try.

I ask Melinda how she knew it was time to make 'Why not now?' part of her mid-life story. 'For most of my adult life,' she begins, 'I've had a pattern of jumping off the proverbial precipice – eyes squeezed shut, palms up – with nothing but blind faith that everything would work out.'

Melinda is the author of four books, an editor, and a speaker. She had spent years helping others share their stories. Empowering people to overcome adversity. Yet, during the COVID lockdown, she found herself re-evaluating her own path. 'I'll acknowledge it was a tough time, but for me, it became one of the happiest periods of my life,' she says. 'I could work from home without the draining commute, and my partner and I created an oasis at home. We cooked new cuisines, took long walks, and really enjoyed our time together.'

But as lockdowns eased, restlessness set in. 'My corporate role no longer felt like 'me'. I'd just turned 50 and wanted more than the nine-to-five grind.' The longing for something more led her and her partner to a bold decision: to move to Queensland's Whitsundays. 'Inspired by childhood holidays to Surfers Paradise, I'd always dreamed of living in Queensland. During an evening walk, we decided to throw caution to the wind and make the leap.'

Once the borders opened, they made the move. 'When we arrived and settled into our new home, everything clicked into place,' she says. 'We built a new community, and suddenly, opportunities started appearing.' Melinda quickly became involved in the local scene, joining the board of the chamber of commerce and reigniting the writers' festival.

Melinda's transformation didn't stop there. 'I started Pilates and loved it so much that I became certified and launched my own business – FIT HIIT Pilates,' she beams. 'I never imagined how much I'd love teaching, and now, my business has even been nominated for a regional award.' Her move from the hustle of city life to a peaceful seaside community marked a new chapter of fulfilment. 'There were challenges,' she admits, 'but they paled in comparison to the joy and revitalisation I've experienced.'

'Being happy in life takes courage,' she says. 'It means letting go of what no longer works, whether it's a career or a relationship. It's not easy, but I promise you – it's worth it.'

If Melinda's story shows us anything, it's that life doesn't wait. It unfolds when you lean into the 'Why not now?' moments and discover that joy is waiting just around the bend. And her tip for us? 'It's the thought I leave with each of my Pilates class participants. Sometimes, the hardest part isn't the leap – it's trusting that the net will appear.' Yes, it is.

Melinda is an editor, writer, speaker, and marketing specialist, and author of four books about eating disorders. She founded FIT HIIT Pilates to empower women to enhance their strength and wellbeing.

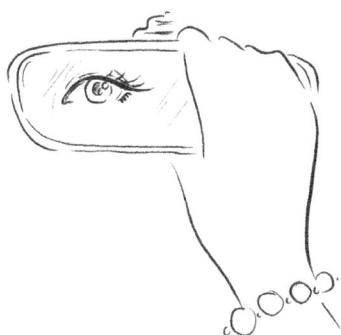

Hello Hindsight – the Gift of Retrospection

After I returned from my travels, I set about applying for every role in my range of expertise and every other role for which I had none. I felt exhilarated, without limits, rebirthed – and then exhausted, crashing into a lather of self-doubt and a sneaking suspicion I was about to become either a parody – a silly older woman with dreams and ideas as yet unfulfilled, and likely to remain that way – or stay on the fence because the 'familiar' is easier. I dug in for some blind faith, and plugged on, researching, reading, stepping outside my comfort zone – until eventually, clarity …

Steering Your Course

One evening, as I scoured Google trying to make sense of this mid-life maelstrom, up popped the work of Murray Stein, a well-known analyst who succinctly sums up my mid-story in the following way:

- The entry point brings a sense of mourning, of racing time.

- What follows is a feeling of wild freedom and joy.

- Then coming home – a full circle back to ourselves with possibility and clarity.

I'm never quite certain if, in hindsight, I wish I knew this stuff. Been forewarned. Or if I should be grateful to have worked through the process. Either way, I neatly 'fit the profile' and now you know what's coming, you may too (or understand the stages you've traversed).

It's comforting to understand a period of feeling lost is almost inevitable. We are simply experiencing another of life's chapters – the magnificence arrives by taking steps to put yourself firmly in the driver's seat and steer a course that suits you.

TRY THIS

Reflect on Murray Stein's outline of mid-life. What stage are you in now?

Start Streamlining Your Lifestyle

The Utmost Importance of Decluttering

Choosing to live in an uncluttered home is the ultimate tool in my wellbeing kit.

By the time I was 21, I had lived in 18 different houses. I'd say that makes me quite the expert on transition. I also learned true comfort and stability does not come from the accumulation of things, but from a deeper connection to the space you inhabit and the treasures you choose to keep.

Instilling a sense of practicality about belongings.

The Beauty of Simplicity

Minimalism isn't about austerity but about making space for what truly matters – from tidying expert Marie Kondo encouraging us to discard 'items that no longer spark joy' to author Margareta Magnusson (*The Gentle Art of Swedish Death Cleaning*) suggesting we declutter our homes not just for our own peace of mind, but also to lessen the load on others after we've gone. There's something deeply comforting about knowing that what remains in your home are the things that truly matter – objects that tell your story, have meaning, and will be received as a gift, not a burden, when bequeathed. A streamlined environment fosters clarity, calm, and a sense of control. It's not just about tidiness; it's about creating a space that supports your wellbeing. When your home is free from excess, it takes less time to maintain, allowing you to focus instead on what's important: your health, your passions, and the people you love. A daily reminder that less can indeed be more, and that true luxury is found in quality, not quantity.

Ask. How many dinner sets do I really need?

Bestow a sense of mindfulness with belongings; for example, try the 'art of tea ceremony' using a fav tea set.

My father relocated countries in his seventies, bequeathing his 'possessions' to my sisters and me – items once precious to him are ours to enjoy while he traverses his later years with a physically (and mentally) lighter load. My grandmother lived by the adage 'never save best for later'. I've taken this on board. Best dresses worn to the supermarket, wedding silver at breakfast, fragrance sprayed at bedtime. Keep what serves you now, release what doesn't. Let your possessions enhance your everyday life, not simply occupy space – beauty in simplicity.

TRY THIS

Set yourself a target of eight weeks to complete clearing clutter. Important: this is a one-person task. Shuffle housemates or family out of the way. You don't want to negotiate; you want to commit to streamlining quickly. Be ruthless. If you don't use an item; flick it, give it, sell it. Done. If you really can't (or don't want to) do this alone, call in a professional declutterer.

Declutter Tech Time Too

I have raised two sons in a fast-paced world of technological advantages – I cannot help but compare their development to my generation. Resilience, attention, communication skills, social networks. I'll save you from my clumsy (and lengthy) assessment of the pros and cons. Instead, I'll share my experiment at downing my phone for a bit.

Dr Danielle Einstein shares expert advice and practical strategies for reducing device use and reclaiming offline time in the next chapter.

My work life has been online for about fifteen years. First a travel blog in early website days, then social media from its inception. I resisted for a moment, wondering how on earth these platforms could ever really catch on – wasn't the point of community to actually be in the presence of other humans, in real life? Well, the rest, as we know, is history. I would do well here to acknowledge the part 'tech' has played in expanding my professional life. When I was a stay-at-home mother, my world shrank. Being online enabled me to grow several businesses beyond my immediate neighbourhood, kept me professionally relevant, and introduced many wonderful people (friends and colleagues). Yet … stepping back from constant connection wasn't just about my phone – it was about making space to be present in a way I hadn't done for years.

Practising Putting it Down

Enroute to an Austrian health retreat, I had an hour to kill at Zurich train station and felt drawn to the small English section in the vast bookshop. Having already decided I should attempt to 'break up' with my phone for stretches whilst ensconced at the retreat (can't very well get to the nub of things constantly scrolling), *Stolen Focus* by Johann Hari stood out from piles of 'easier' reads. It should have been perfect – to sit with a book about lack of focus as I sort to still my mind and be with my thoughts. Yet the past few years had rendered me unable to enjoy a previous love of reading beyond an 'easy novel'. Ever the optimist, I bought it.

Something about the fresh air, hours spent in nature, evening yoga, mindful nutrition meant *Stolen Focus* took a backseat – although, so too my phone. When I eventually read the book upon my return home, it did encourage yet another reconnection with disconnection. *Occasionally*, I leave my phone at home so I am forced to stand in a queue, not have noise in my ears, be comfortable in my own thoughts. Did it feel uncomfortable at first? YES – and I noticed how little we now connect, make eye contact – faces constantly down. It is cathartic (and empowering) to know we can be in charge of our own impulses still.

Expert: Dr Danielle Einstein – Positively Disconnecting

'Dr Einstein, you began your psychology career caring for patients with anxiety. At what point did you note the correlation with these conditions and the tech world – and what can we individually do to address this?'

Dr Danielle Einstein: 'As soon as children had their parent's old phones, especially when they were hand-me-down smartphones (circa 2012), all of a sudden, children had the ability to share. There's been a conundrum ever since about how much help to give and when to give it. Phones have been invaluable for parents juggling multiple demands, but they have also allowed teens to reach out quickly when they encounter a problem. On the other hand, our children's worlds have been rocked by social media and its ability to spread every mistake like wildfire before they had the maturity to deal with the fallout wisely. Our kids need a solid sense of who they are and how to cope with a range of situations, and their own emotions, before they are let loose on social media.'

Let's zoom out to think about wider tech use for us in mid-life. Without realising it, technology can be a temptress, thieving our time second by second and undermining quality. Tech use can stealthily undermine priorities if you don't have a tight hold on it. Positively disconnecting involves recognising the role of dopamine and its connection with the sounds your device emits and the places you pull out your tech, whether that be your bed, couch or other rooms at home. Dopamine is powerful, and the more you give yourself, the more you crave.

Social media may lift your mood, but by and large, social media has a negative effect. Why? Because we can't control how others react to us in group situations. You may have built an audience, developed a tough skin, and become resilient to rejection over many years. The kick we receive when we see emojis and positive comments in our feed is well-studied, and it keeps us coming back for more. The question is, how do we separate that from reality and avoid becoming over reliant on the online community for our sense of self?

If we are in this trap, it may be hard to resist the temptation to pick up a phone in front of others ('phone snubbing' is the technical term). You may not be aware that having your phone on the table upside down in front of you lowers your fluid intelligence (your ability to think on your feet) compared to when it is in your bag or another room. Out of sight is the key. You don't need studies to remind you that real life is where the best connections are found.

Dr Danielle Einstein is a Clinical Psychologist who works with adolescents and parents, and an Adjunct Fellow at Macquarie University. Her research examines the connection between anxiety and digital wellbeing. She offers practical resources for redirecting teen and parent worry through www.danielleeinstein.com. In 2024, she co-authored Raising Anxiety: Why our good intentions are backfiring on children (and how to fix it) *with parenting expert Dr Judith Locke.*

TRY THIS

Dr Einstein's advice: put all social media on one device and use it, if possible, in one location in your home. Avoid the bedroom. Check the amount of time you spend on it each day. Unfollow anyone who negatively impacts your wellbeing. One research study suggested that if you fall into the comparison trap regularly, you feel worse if you follow strangers than if you follow friends. We all know that some friends bring out a sense of competition and comparison. Dr Einstein's solution: communicate with those you like one-to-one rather than through social media. One-to-one friendships give back through quality time and depth of understanding. Communication doesn't have to be frequent; it needs to be trusting and open if you want to enrich mid-life. Consider a physical timer if you are digesting news online and continually fall for the hyperlink-after-hyperlink drawcard. Lastly, if you check emails too much, remove them from your phone.

How to (Start to) Feel Reinvigorated

Diary Note …

Lately, there's been a creeping flabbiness – not just over my frame, though that's there too, but in the shape of my days. Some glide by with purpose, others leave me treading water. And in the pecking order of family life? Let's just say I'm somewhere near the bottom, itching to shake things up.

Yesterday, on my usual walk, I passed a group of older women ambling along the beachfront, laughing with that deep, glorious kind of joy – the kind that plants a spring in your step. They had years on me, but you wouldn't know it from the way they moved. I couldn't help thinking, I want whatever they're having.

The Next Day...

This morning, before the house stirred, I slipped out quietly and headed to the beach. The July air biting, and the lone swimmer looked like a distant, brave soul. For a moment, I hesitated – until I thought of those women from yesterday. They had looked like they would have the nerve; surely I could muster some too.

The cold sea as horrific as I'd imagined – freezing, breath gasping. A few tentative strokes and my body adjusted to the chilling swell, and into the blue I swam. Hardly an Arctic expedition, but I felt like a bloody legend – and free. Through my goggles, a forgotten world: fish darting beneath me, the tides shifting the sand. It hit me: real change starts when we make space for it – not with grand gestures, but by showing up daily, even in small ways. Today, it's just the beginning, a fresh start. A frisson of excitement for what now may come. Oh, joy, a bit of wild came out to play!

Feeling Better Feels (Nothing Beats It)

Feeling better – in whichever form that takes for you – is inevitably where many mid-life conversations lead. Springing out of bed is perhaps a distant fantasy – yet there is plenty you can do to move the needle on your lifestyle to start to see positive results. Unfortunately, we cannot click our fingers and one day miraculously find a magic 'Open here for your immediate body and mind change' box on our doorstep.

After decades of structuring my lifestyle around wellbeing and working with women to implement the practices, I've realised three overarching truths to living life in optimum wellbeing:

- No one path looks the same.

- A reckoning is essential for real change.

- Enduring results don't come from quick fixes.

This chapter answers a simple question: What can I do today to move the needle toward feeling better?

Breakout

A sense of wellbeing isn't a gift; it can't be bequeathed. It must be built – layer by layer – by you, for you.

When I need to reset, I go back to basics. If I can follow these steps, anyone can. My natural habitat as a kid was under a doona, struggling to breathe through asthma, reading a book, and eating crisps. Nothing about this lifestyle came naturally to me. I just choose feeling great over feeling average.

Feeling better is about retreating within – getting quiet enough to listen. We'll dive deeper in future chapters, but this section is your place to start.

Five Days, Five Things, Feel Better

If five things feel overwhelming, just try one. Start tonight with 30 minutes more sleep. Or have lunch tomorrow without checking your phone. These shifts may seem small, but they carry real weight.

1. SLEEP

- Get more sleep than you think you need. Sleep fuels everything that's ahead – fun on the horizon, yes, but it'll take effort.
- Tonight: Aim for 30 more minutes than usual.

2. WEAR

- Tomorrow morning, wear clothes that make you feel great. You deserve to look as good as you feel.
- Mantra: *Best foot(wear) forward – confidence isn't waiting in your activewear.*

3. MOVE

- If you don't have a daily routine, start with 10 minutes of movement three times a day.
- Ideas: Walk around the block, followed by 10 squats, 10 push-ups, 10 lunges, 10 tricep dips.
- Mantra: *Start with weight-bearing movements, then build in balance and flexibility practices.*

The benefit of just a ten-minute walk after meals cannot be underestimated.

4. EAT

- Eat mindfully, with no distractions unless dining with loved ones.

- Ideas: Put down cutlery between bites; no tech for company.
- Struggling with weight? Kickstart with five days of simple, nutritious meals. Prep the same meals every day – focus on whole, unprocessed food.
- Pro tip: Avoid fake foods, juice fasts, or overly complicated plans. A quick detox can be helpful – but keep it simple.
- Tea recipe (for when cravings hit), add hot water to:
  - ◆ Chopped fresh ginger
  - ◆ Fresh mint and lemon
  - ◆ Honey to taste

Reaching for something you can't stop eating (hello, jelly sweeties)? Say: '(Insert your name), eating this today won't feel great later.' (Borrowed from author Elizabeth Gilbert).

5. MINDSET

- If meditation feels daunting, start with a walk in nature. It can work just as well to clear your mind.
- Mantra: *Nature every day – because when I follow my own advice, the rest flows.*

In five days, you'll feel refreshed and better – and that's the start.

You have this. You really do.

Finding Yourself Again

Synchronicity brought Prue Francis and I into each other's orbit. Her decision to introduce herself gave weight to my once-tentative thoughts of turning my musings into this guidebook – and for that, I'm profoundly grateful.

I first met Prue in Airlie Beach during her sailing trip to the Whitsundays. 'Escaping the winter chill with friends was just the tonic I needed,' she tells me. Prue grew up on a cattle and horse stud in rural NSW, where she developed a love for the land and community, a grounding that would influence her later life. Now co-owner of an agricultural consultancy in Wagga Wagga, she balances managing the business with raising her three children.

If you feel pulled, always say that 'HELLO' and make a connection; you never know where it might lead!

At the end of her holiday, Prue decided to visit a local boutique I'd recommended on Instagram (the algorithms had popped her in my orbit). Randomly I strolled in as she arrived. 'I recognised you instantly,' she recalls. 'I almost hesitated to introduce myself, but I really wanted to share how much your story resonated. After we chatted you took a photo of us together – our spontaneous encounter ignited something in me.'

At that time, Prue was feeling lost. 'I felt puffy, overwhelmed, tired, and lonely,' she admits. With her husband often away for work, eldest son on with his life, her middle son on a gap year, and her youngest at boarding school, she had expected a sense of freedom. 'But instead of joy, I felt like I had a huge hole in my heart. I was confused and missed the person I was when I was busy with family life.'

After the holiday, Prue knew she needed a change. 'I started prioritising myself,' she says, 'focusing on eating better and exercising.' Her doctor prescribed HRT for perimenopause, which made a significant difference. 'My sleep, mood, and energy levels all improved,' she adds, grateful for the openness of her generation about mid-life challenges.

'A book club with close friends has been a lifesaver,' Prue continues. 'It's a non-judgmental community of women who share openly. We take turns hosting and cooking, and it's one of the most grounding parts of my life.'

Reflecting on her journey from rural NSW to business owner, mother, and someone rediscovering herself, Prue shares her insight: 'The key is embracing life's twists and turns. Prioritising time for yourself, finding meaningful work, nurturing friendships, and surrounding yourself with love – those are the foundations of my happy, balanced life.'

Prue Francis grew up on a cattle and horse stud in NSW and now co-owns an agricultural consultancy in Wagga Wagga. She credits her book club crew, friends, the chance meeting with Monique, and her family with inspiring her ongoing growth and reflection.

Motherlode and Finances: The Truth of the Matter

The 'unpaid and unrecognised domestic labour' of mothers and carers – and resulting lack of sufficient superannuation and assets for many women – cannot be ignored around our mid-life conversation.

It is nigh impossible to 'play catch up'. When my 76-year-old mother divorced several decades ago, superannuation was not even on the table, resulting in a leaner retirement than commensurate with her stay-at-home sacrifice and later business success. She suggests, tongue in cheek, 'Until men can have babies, not much will change'. Perhaps.

I was financially independent until I wasn't. I felt for many years beholden, childish, and stuck. Privileged but caged. As soon as I had children, I became, for the most part, a full-time mum, my professional aspirations token and cobbled around family needs. I am exceedingly fortunate my spluttering income wasn't required to feed our family, releasing immeasurable pressure not afforded to all. Additionally, I was able to carve out time periodically to recharge my batteries – so by the time my sons reached 'end-of-school years', I had a modicum of energy left. Good use of that vigour is to my determination to continue this conversation for as long as it takes for it to be taken seriously, for all of us.

The Domestic Divide

Whilst researching this book, I listened to Anna Funder on the *Wild with Sarah Wilson* podcast, discussing her mid-life malaise while juggling deadlines and groceries. It hit home. I gleaned it was, in part, her frustration with the invisible load women carry that inspired her to write her book *Wifedom*. For me, running away from my family was a different, but no less real, response to that same imbalance.

I acknowledge I am a middle-class woman with an enormously fortunate life, a husband, and children I love. The luxury of being able to afford to be in and out of work to take on the majority of our household domestics makes me 'lucky'. Still, this sticks in my craw. I am certain my husband and I discussed the division of domestics early on in our relationship. I took that as a desire to 'share' parenting, advance our careers while our children were well cared for, and make all-important time for each other as a couple. In retrospect, what it meant in reality was that a lack of childcare options resulted in my interrupted career – not his. Unfortunately, for many mid-life women, this was 'the way it was'.

Our social construct is such that, without systemic change, it seems there is little we can do individually. Not confined to an

'Australian issue' (although traditionally slow to move the dial on the 'male as breadwinner' model), globally, women continue to do more unpaid domestic labour (housework, caring for kids, older relatives) and arrange careers around families (fewer hours, lower status roles), resulting in reduced superannuation and other benefits of career longevity (money, housing security).

Raising children must be more valued and the skills required to keep the show on the road acknowledged and subscribed monetary value. As the CEO of the Association of Superannuation Funds Australia, Churchill Fellow, and champion for gender equity in superannuation, Mary Delahunty is recognised for her research on retirement outcomes. With expertise in ESG and responsible investment, her career reflects a dedication to strengthening retirement outcomes for Australians. Her valuable contribution to the conversation:

'Taking a break to 'care' should not put you backwards financially, especially when we are producing beautiful little future taxpayers.'

Yes!

Do Not Dig Your Head in the (Financial Literacy) Sand

Financial literacy and good management allow for options, freedom, generosity, and security. To my detriment, I allowed my skills in finance to lay dormant for several decades – I am ashamed to state that I 'dug my head in the financial literacy sand'. I am brilliant at stretching a dollar, making a silk purse out of a sow's ear, spending several uni years eating two-minute noodles on repeat (to save for travel), maintaining a household on a budget, yadda yadda. It's simply the nuances of investing that eluded me. I could easily have ended up a financial mess but for the guidance of more astute family members. I am not alone.

CEO of Your Finances

Now we've explored some of the deeper challenges surrounding unpaid labour and financial literacy, it's time to become the **CEO of your finances**. We need to talk openly about money. Conversations about budgets, investments, and savings shouldn't be rare or embarrassing – women need to be part of the financial dialogue. Sobering studies like *The Future Face of Poverty is Female* remind us of the stakes.

Find someone in your circle to talk finances with – whether they're ahead or behind where you are. These chats don't need to be detailed strategy sessions, just honest conversations that open the door to greater literacy. Sometimes, we need a sounding board to figure out the next step. For the deep dives? Find a good financial adviser or accountant.

I enlisted the help of experts Melissa Browne (finance) and Michelle van Tulder (property). Observant readers will note her surname – she is my clever, financially astute younger sister, the ex-HR and legal director of one of Sir Richard Branson's companies. Do not skip their chapters.

Financial literacy underpins a life of wellbeing – seek qualified professional support if you know your stress and wellbeing will not improve without getting a handle on what you do, or do not, have in the bank.

TRY THIS

The ASFA Retirement Standard, produced quarterly by the Association of Superannuation Funds Australia (ASFA), is a great way to get a handle on how much money you might need to live on in the future. Then start to **plan**. There are reputable and accredited businesses focused on women's money matters with loads of online resources.

Expert: Melissa Browne – Finance 101

MvT: 'What remains is 'the truth of the matter': too many mid-life women are left feeling wobbly about finances. Help!'

Melissa: 'It's easy to be ambivalent or hope you're doing enough when 'life is good'. But when life happens, whether through illness, losing your job, divorce, hitting a particular age, or simply trying to navigate rising inflation, interest rates, and economic uncertainty – popping your head in the sand isn't a sound financial strategy. That's when many of us realise we need to 'financially adult'. If you are prepared to unlearn any previous blocks around finances, then it is possible to 'relearn' to shape your future, be more financially in control, and importantly, take action.'

When Life Happens

As mid-life women, many of us have been multitasking queens – balancing work, family, ageing parents and everything in between. Yet when it comes to our finances, too many of us feel wobbly, uncertain, and unsure where to start. The financial realities of mid-life can hit hard. A nagging sense that we should have it figured out by now – a solid retirement plan, a robust savings account, and an investment portfolio that's working for us. However, life has a way of throwing curveballs. Perhaps you took time off work to raise your children or care for a loved one, or maybe a divorce or job loss has thrown your financial plans off course. You might be staring at your bank statements or superannuation balance, feeling like time is not on your side to make up for the lost earning potential of those years.

I'm here to say it's not too late to learn how to design your best financial future.

Be the Main Character in YOUR Finance Story

The world of finance can seem daunting, filled with jargon, numbers, and strategies that feel as foreign as a language you've never studied. It's little wonder you feel that way – most of us didn't have a 'finance' class at school or didn't talk about money at home. The first thing to recognise is that financial literacy is a skill that can be learned at any age. Whether you're 15, 45, or 85, you have the ability to build your financial knowledge and make informed decisions about your money. I want you to run out of excuses, not money. I want you to bring main character energy into your finances, to not let someone else be driving while you are asleep on the back seat (or hiding in the boot).

The Emotional Hurdle

One of the biggest barriers to taking control of your finances is the emotional hurdle. Fear of the unknown, of making mistakes, and fear of discovering your financial situation might not be as secure as you'd hoped can all hold you back. But remember, these feelings are normal, and don't have to prevent you from moving forward.

Acknowledge these fears, but don't let them paralyse you. Instead, use them as motivation to take action. The more you learn about your finances, the less intimidating they will become. You don't need to do it all at once – small, consistent steps will build your confidence over time. Even if it's three steps forward and two back, it's about the gradual forward momentum.

Taking control of your finances is not just about securing your future, it's about knowing that you are capable of managing your money and creating the financial future you want. It's never too late to learn, to take action, and make a difference in your financial life. Start feeling empowered. You've got this.

TRY THIS

1. Do a Financial Health Check

The first step is to face where you currently stand. Gather all your financial documents – bank statements, superannuation statements, insurance policies, debts – and understand where you're starting from. What you're earning, what expenses are going out, what you have, and what you owe. It might feel overwhelming and confronting, but it's essential. If you're unsure where to start, seek help from a financial counsellor, a financial educator like me, or a financial planner (depending on your budget and capacity).

2. Educate Yourself

Financial literacy isn't something you're born with or study at school (sadly) – it's something you learn. Read books, listen to finance podcasts, or join my Financial Adulting Course designed to not only educate you but also help you create a financial plan you're excited about. And don't be afraid to ask questions. The more you know, the more confident you'll be in making decisions. Seek out resources tailored specifically to women's financial needs, as they often address the unique challenges we face.

3. Automate and Simplify Your Finances

Life is busy enough without adding extra stress. Automate managing your finances:

- Automatic transfers to savings or investment accounts.

- Automate bill payments and simplify your financial life.

- Consider consolidating superannuation accounts to reduce fees.

Create a routine for reviewing your finances regularly – weekly check-ins or monthly reviews – to keep yourself engaged and on track.

Melissa Browne is an ex-financial adviser and bestselling author empowering women to achieve financial independence and turning her journey from financial struggle to inspiration. Through her books, speaking, and the My Financial Adulting Plan. Melissa encourages women to transform their financial lives and pursue personal and professional growth with confidence.

Expert: Michelle van Tulder – A Thing or Two About Your Abode

MvT: 'Michelle, given our homes may well be the largest part of our portfolios, how might we maximise our investments in mid-life?'

Michelle: 'Property – bricks and mortar – is many things. At one end, you have endless dinner party conversations on what you should have bought and when. Maybe you debate between saving for retirement through shares or houses, perhaps you enjoy scouring the internet for that perfect home. At the other end, you have problems financing repairs on your house, splitting the marital home, or downsizing as children take flight. Wherever you find yourself in the property space, one common area that most will agree on is that property is more than just four walls and a roof. It contains everything you hold dear. So, with that in mind, let's take stock.'

I am debt-free on my home to plan for my retirement. If yes, skip this chapter and go to the top of the class!

My children have left home, and I spend endless days dusting empty, silent corners. If yes, let's explore downsizing or tenanting that extra space. If you want to stay put and need extra spending money, consider renting out a room. In many countries, this can create a tax advantage, as you are running a business and can claim the costs of running your home against the rental income. Depending on your location, you could rent to a person who is there for business during the week so you have your home to yourself on weekends, or you could offer short-term accommodation for tourists. The possibilities are many; it's a matter of designing something that works for you.

I am parting company with my partner. If yes, you need to work out how best to run two households, which is more complicated if there are children involved. Getting a handle on your finances and property is a key component. You might be required to rent as you wait for settlement and will be looking at options substantially smaller or in a less desirable neighbourhood than previously. It will be okay as long as you face this dilemma head-on. This is the time to have an honest think about what you have and what you can afford going forward. An opportunity for reinvigoration and renewal.

I am renting and worried that it is too late to get on the property ladder. If yes, it is time to dust off your spreadsheeting skills. Review your financial inflows and outflows to see the amount you have left to save. For some, buying property has not been a priority or possibility. That is okay; it is not for everyone. What we need is stability. Make sure that you have enough coming in to cover your rent and other expenses. Are you able to negotiate a long-term rental reduction if you don't need to move? Just because you are renting, it doesn't make you powerless – a stable tenant is of value to a landlord. Check your ability to meet rent long-term and take your power back!

I am selling my property. If yes, in many cases, this is the easiest tax-free money you will ever make. The trick to maximising your sales value comes down to many things you cannot control.

The economic cycle, interest rates, governments, the weather (seriously!), your circumstances. However, there are other factors that can help influence your buyer. Your job, as a seller, is to become a dream weaver. Consider having your home professionally styled, declutter each space, depersonalise your environment by removing or hiding personal belongings and putting new linen on your bed, refresh your garden with mulch. Find a local agent with a proven track record in your area and a reputable lawyer. Get hold of your appliance warranties, planning permission, insurance documents, title details, and anything else your lawyer will need.

I am buying a home. If yes, it is worth investing time to think about the best way to proceed. Run your numbers and work out how much you can afford. If you need a mortgage, 'stress test' the interest rates. A good mortgage broker can help. Use your head, not your heart – treat this purchase like a business transaction. A new property purchase should have a medium-term time frame. Think about who is living with you now and the longevity. Are you buying as an empty-nester? Newly divorced? Single with no intention of sharing your wardrobe, let alone your bed, again? We cannot plan for everything, but it is useful to take an honest look at your current living arrangements.

Your home is your castle, and it can be stressful during mid-life to reassess many things at once. It is important to ensure that you are in a strong mental and physical space to make such a change. Even if you are not quite ready, going through the ideas in this chapter can help you draft a plan towards your ultimate goal: a healthy, content and financially independent self, inhabiting your best space.

TRY THIS

Courtesy of decades of property learnings, let's recap:

1. Ask yourself if you are living in the right home for today (and for the next five to ten years).
2. Review your finances to ensure that you can afford your home for the short to medium term.
3. If you need to change your home, invest in getting it ready for sale, maximising the sale price.
4. Engage professionals to help you realise your property goals.

With over 25 years in prime central London residential property, Michelle van Tulder excels at maximising property values, connecting high-net-worth individuals with top-tier professionals. When not immersed in property, Michelle is writing – her first fiction book, Table 72: The Girl Without a Filter, *is set in vibrant Chelsea, London.*

Breakout

I have seen too many people alter their lifestyle to a seemingly more fabulous 'tree or sea change' existence, which it could well be in the short term. Yet they have no plan for later, when priorities might change. A desire to live amongst swaying palm trees in your fifties may give way to a need for proximity to healthcare and family in your seventies. Use mid-life to consider the safety net that may be needed in future decades.

Why, What, How – The Roadmap

How We're Going to Get Where We're Going

Think of this roadmap as your North Star – not a strict path but a guide to navigating mid-life with clarity and intention.

1. Your Why – Identify Your Values (*What anchors you?*)

- **Reflect.** What truly matters to you? What do you stand for?
- **Choose 3–5 core values.** What ideals serve as your personal compass?
- **Look for patterns.** Review past choices – what themes or values emerge?
- **Feel your values.** How do you want to feel? (e.g. confident, connected, peaceful)

Action Step: Play with a list of values and narrow it down to 3–5 that feel most essential. Keep them visible as a reminder of what grounds you.

2. Your What – Design Your Mid-Life Anthem (*What resonates with the life you want to live now?)*

- **Define fulfilment.** What does mid-life success or joy look like for you?
- **Align with values.** How can your vision reflect your core values?
- **Look back.** What past passions or goals are calling to be revisited?

Action Step: Write three simple goals or experiences you want to feel or achieve in the near future. Let these be your compass points for the next phase.

3. Your How – Take Action (*Start small, move forward.)*

- **Start with one simple action.** Choose a small step that aligns with your vision.
- Build healthy habits.
- **Cue.** What will trigger the habit?
- **Routine.** Make it easy and doable.
- **Reward.** What will make it satisfying?
- **Reassess weekly.** Adjust as needed based on what feels right.

Action Step: Choose one beneficial habit or action to start this week – something that feels manageable but meaningful.

Perhaps What You Really Need Is Purpose

Living On Purpose

Purpose, or your personal 'why', isn't about arriving at an endpoint but is about movement – an ongoing journey. It's what gives meaning to our lives, keeps us curious, and provides direction. The now well-documented Blue Zones (more on these regions in a moment) are home to many healthy centenarians who live with an innate sense of purpose. In Okinawa, Japan, it's called *ikigai* – reason for being – and in Nicoya, Costa Rica, it's known as *plan de vida* – a life plan. In both cases, it's about leading a life anchored in meaningful pursuits.

TRY THIS

Are you living in alignment with your values now? What could change?

Suggested viewing: the Blue Zones documentary.

I encourage a value-led lifestyle, with purpose and action at the forefront of daily decisions by always asking: 'What is your *raison d'être?*' – your reason for being (in mid-life). This approach intersects beautifully with positive psychology, which emphasises meaning and the pursuit of a life worth living. Both this and Ikigai philosophies guide you toward living with intention and creating a mid-life filled with purpose.

For further reading, *Flourish* by Martin Seligman for positive psychology and *Ikigai: The Japanese Secret to a Long and Happy Life* by Héctor García and Francesc Miralles.

Why Discovering Your Why Matters

Finding purpose isn't easy. A lull can creep in, creating indecision – *What if this is the wrong direction? What if I don't like it?* These moments make clarity feel elusive.

Do you know what you value – the core of your existence, the shape of a life well-lived? Your *why*? I'm not certain I had ever fully crystallised what I stood for. I had an intrinsic sense of what lit me up, what I wouldn't tolerate – from myself or others – and what I viewed as right and wrong. If someone had pressed me, I might have called them my morals. Morals are taught by society, but values are discovered within. And that journey of discovery is lifelong. And your why? Well, that's where your values and purpose meet.

At this point, it's easy to disappear down the rabbit hole and end up more confused than when you began. So, let's skip the existential spiral and get practical. This isn't about woo – it's about:

- Who you are
- What you want
- Why you want 'it'

… for your second act. And then we'll talk behaviours – How you're going to live it. Remember, this is a direction, not a destination. A work in progress.

When I finally did the exercise below, I noticed a pattern. Sure, circumstances forced choices. Things important to me were set aside to keep the proverbial show on the road. But still, the people

I gravitate toward, the man I married, the way we raised our boys – all of these decisions flowed from a core set of guiding principles. My values compass, if you will. When I saw that, the lightbulb switched on.

In summary, here are my top six values, the ones I hold in the highest regard:

authenticity, connection, curiosity, freedom, optimism, wellbeing.

Wellbeing sits firmly at the top. If I'm not strong, fit, and well-nourished – if I haven't slept properly – my world tilts off its axis. I could add more, like *adventurous*, but honestly, *curiosity* and a desire for *connection* are what bring the excitement. I don't seek adventure for the sake of it; it's simply a byproduct of living true to my core values. Same with *wisdom* – while I enjoy feeling wise with experience, I don't exactly leap out of bed with a burning need to 'spread my wise'.

TRY THIS

Start with choosing 3–5 values – an abridged list below – that sum up your non-negotiables. It's time to get clear on what you value, so you can start making choices that align.

A quick google search will bring forth a myriad of more complete values lists

Some ideas to get you started:

Authenticity, adventure, community, connection, courage, curiosity, health and fitness, freedom, leadership, optimism, security, self-respect, spirituality, success, wellbeing, wisdom.

Aligning Life with Values

When a decision is required – personal or professional, I filter it through the lens of my values. Does it allow me to be authentic? Will it foster connection? Does it spark curiosity, or align with wellbeing? Does it grant me the freedom I cherish? If the answer is yes, I move forward confidently. If not, I know it's not for me.

What You Actually Like to Do

Knowing your values is step one. Aligning your choices with them is where the magic happens. A great way to begin? Look back to move forward. Answer these:

- What did you love doing as a child or teen – before life got complicated?
- What activities put you in a state of 'flow'?
- Are there forgotten moments or sliding-door decisions that shaped your life?
- What aspects of your adult work life felt most rewarding?

I'll share:

1. Growing up with entrepreneurial parents, I spent weekends immersed in our family business. I learned early that storytelling wasn't just about words – it connected customers with products. My pocket money came from handing out business cards – dealing with rejection and PR from the start!

   Realisation: I love storytelling – it's the core of what I do today. Resilience is in my DNA; I have bounce-back in spades.

2. Weekends were spent skiing, sailing, and hiking off-grid. Life was lived outdoors, with farm-to-table food. Mum and Dad, the original 'Bear Grylls'.

   Realisation: nature remains essential to my wellbeing. I thrive in action, not stillness.

3. As a newly arrived student in high school, I campaigned for a role on the student council. What I understood instinctively was the power to question and listen. I landed the VP role.

Realisation: it's the intent to actively listen that creates space and leads clients to success. I love being a conduit.

Deliver what people want, not what you think they need.

The Tough Questions

Self-reflection can unlock clarity and get you unstuck. Ask yourself:

*   What are your secret strengths – the things you breeze through while others struggle?

*   Who's on your responsibility list, and how do you juggle them without neglecting yourself?

*   If you dared to shake things up, how would your life look on the other side?

*   What's driving the itch for change?

Remember, this process is fluid – your answers will shift as you gain greater awareness of what you want. Come up with simple, achievable ideas for each question and write them in your notebook. Let the answers marinate for a while, then see what emerges.

Designing Your Mid-Life Anthem

Your dream vision for the future is deeply personal – whether it's sitting in the sun with a great book surrounded by family or returning to professional life. Whatever it is, stay true to your core values as you design a life that works for you. The moment dreams become reality is magnificent, but the anticipation is equally beguiling. Visualisation techniques work – they're not just 'woo woo'.

A dream doesn't have to be grand – sometimes it's a small intention that grows into something bigger. Mine began as a random thought, serendipity raising her hand. After I had determined to commit to making wellbeing changes, I spotted an image of a wellness retreat in a magazine, clocking it as 'somewhere I'd really, really like to be right now'. Later that day, I passed our local MECCA store, where the same retreat's founder beamed down from a poster advertising her holistic skincare range.

A random sidebar I forgot: Dad reminded me later that, 12 months prior, he had sent me an article about the retreat, thinking 'I might like it'. Freaky.

At the time, taking 'time out' wasn't immediately possible (kids at school – oh, and we were in the middle of COVID and not moving further than our street). If it had been, I would have run off to find that elusive space first. Instead, I began by building strength and getting healthier. I stuck a picture of that retreat in the Austrian Alps on my bedroom mirror – but I am not certain I actually thought I would ever be walking in their front door as it might as well have been Mars (yup, I chose a place thousands of kilometres from my home in Sydney – talk about lofty vision). Nevertheless, all the while, that picture gave me a dream of sorts.

Without that dream – and unconsciously reconnecting with my values – this book might never have existed. All the gloriousness that followed may never have unfolded, and upon reflection, that's deeply unsettling.

There's no 'complete roadmap' for life, and the route to clarity can feel convoluted. Oh, I got there in the end, but who knows if, armed with what I know now, I'd have taken a different path. Seeing backwards isn't one of my gifts – but seeing forward? Now that I can help you with.

TRY THIS

You don't need a whole vision board. I just needed one picture stuck on my vanity mirror. Your dream, your vision, your way – do keep it front and centre, alongside your list of values. When the going gets tough, it'll give you a boost.

How to Design Your Next Act

If you don't like the road you are walking, start paving another one.

– Dolly Parton.

Now that you've identified your values and your vision, it's time to act. Think of this as an experiment – take small steps toward your ideal future, even if it's messy.

TRY THIS: Ask yourself.

- If I were the ideal version of myself, what would I be doing?
- I would like to ... (feel, transform, achieve ...)
- So that I may ... (live fully, thrive, do some things differently...)

How Do You Want to Feel?

Type these up, tape them to your mirror, and revisit them often. Stretch with a dream, but be realistic about the execution. There's no point saying, 'I'd like to float around the Mediterranean on a superyacht,' if one of your values is supporting your ageing mum. Instead, be honest about your circumstances.

You can always book a day cruise close to home.

Often, we arrive with a shopping list of what we think we want, but once we shed the excess, it becomes clear that what we're really chasing is a feeling:

- To feel more in tune with my values
- To feel more confident
- To feel more balanced
- To feel happier in my current life situation
- To feel stronger so I can be more adventurous
- To sleep better so I have more energy
- To eat well so I have the nutrients my body needs

- To feel more connected, loved, seen, heard
- To reinvigorate my personal branding – 'look' and 'feel' more like me
- To feel more courageous
- To feel more streamlined in life – home, finances, commitments

When you align your internal and external surroundings with what you want to attract, synchronicity tends to appear.

I remain true to my values by consistently reassessing my lifestyle.

1. Pillars of wellbeing – community, nutrition, movement, mindfulness, sleep, purpose.

2. Regularly reinvigorate my personal branding. This plays into the above point and includes looking on point and full of vitality.

This is not a shallow aspiration – it does matter, and I'll expand on this later.

3. To feel more confident. I lean into 'Why not now' and 'Why not me?' – as opportunities arise, if they align with my values, I go for it.

TRY THIS

Choose three feelings that resonate with you. What action could you take to achieve them?

So, How to Move Forward?

No-one wakes up ready to climb Everest, expecting to have all the tools in place on day one. No business is an overnight success – there are usually years of hard work behind the scenes. The same goes for losing weight, getting fit, building mindfulness, reawakening your professional life, or cleaning up your finances. It all takes time, planning, and effort.

Baby Steps, Baby

You can't just imagine the future and will it into being. Your current situation may make it seem impossible, but that's where baby steps come in. Small, bite-sized movements will get you going – one step at a time.

It's incredibly rewarding to make progress – and daunting. You may find it far easier to think about doing something rather than actually doing it. Trust me, I'm a seasoned mistress of 'perfecting' before 'starting'. Convincing yourself that you'll get to it someday, only to berate yourself later for not starting, is far more exhausting than simply beginning. Procrastination is like trying to push a shopping cart with a wonky wheel – it's frustrating, gets you nowhere, and makes everything take twice as long.

The trick?

There isn't one. Action beats perfection every single time.

You don't need to have everything figured out. What you need is to start – messy, imperfect, and unsure.

Baby steps, baby.

TRY THIS

This is the stepped habit formation technique as author James Clear outlines in *Atomic Habits*.

Maybe you want to take a trekking retreat six months from now, and you know your fitness isn't there, yet – what needs to happen is for you to begin to walk regularly. But it is hard to carve out the time amidst everything else the day requires of you.

Cue: Make it obvious. Lay out your gear the night before.

Craving: Make it attractive. Save your favourite podcast to only listen to on your walk.

Response: Make it easy. Just 15 minutes around the block.

Reward: Make it satisfying. Track your progress and celebrate wins.

Plan for curveballs. Raining? Grab an umbrella. Rough night? Remind yourself it's only 15 minutes.

Habits take about 12 weeks to stick – but that's a far-off number. Focus on the next two weeks, and then repeat. Review your progress every Sunday and stretch yourself when you're ready.

When I get Bored with the Sh+t I Tell Myself…

Breaking habits isn't easy, but staying stuck is harder. My sugar habit is a perfect example – I'd detour through the supermarket for sweets, feel bliss for five minutes, then regret it for hours. I didn't quit as a hard stop. I swapped sweets for a square of dark chocolate – just enough to satisfy without the guilt. The trick is pausing, reassessing, and pivoting when needed.

Discovering Confidence: The Mid-Life Silver Lining

Diary Note…

I could have chosen a quieter way to rediscover my confidence – something subtle, away from scrutiny. Instead, a media training day popped up in my Instagram feed, led by Shelly Horton (media maven and menopause warrior) and Tory Archbold (women's empowerment powerhouse). That familiar voice whispered, 'What the hell are you thinking?' but I booked it anyway.

The morning of, every logical instinct screamed, *'Turn back!'* But I pulled myself together, game face on, and stepped into a room of polished women who *seemed* to have it all figured out. Within an hour, the illusion shattered – behind the perfect outfits and professional polish were similar doubts I carried. Am I good enough? Will I look foolish? Many of us steering the same rickety boat, navigating the messy waters of life.

What I Learned from My Mid-Life Baptism by Camera

As I often remind my sons: *People care about you, but no-one is watching as closely as you think.*

I cried on camera – tears for the nonsense that held me back, for chasing 'stuff' that didn't matter. In that moment – a lightness, a release.

- **Everyone's faking it.** We're all grappling with the same doubts and doing the best we can.

- **Vulnerability is liberating.** The moment we stop chasing perfection, we realise we're never alone in our struggles.

132

- **The inner critic lies.** That voice insisting you're not enough? It's a liar. You *are* enough. Psychologists describe 'feeling less than' as a mental loop that convinces us we're not enough – yet 70% of people experience it at some point, especially during periods of transition.

Later, watching the footage, I noticed my usual critic creeping in: I nodded too much. My shirt colour wrong. *Who am I to proffer advice when I don't have all the answers?* But here's the shift: I no longer have the energy for that tired old story. There's nothing left to prove, only permission to move forward.

And the truth? Life rarely aligns perfectly. Waiting for the right moment is exhausting – but small, intentional steps can fling off that cloak of doubt.

TRY THIS: Ask what's holding you back

- *I've never achieved anything of note.*

- *I'm too old to start fresh, find a new job, or travel solo.*

- *I'll start once I … lose weight, have more time, or the kids grow up.*

Instead of waiting, list ten things you *have* accomplished. Include everything from parenting milestones to career successes – even the quirky childhood ones. My mum still praises me for being a champion swimmer … at 15. But her enthusiasm encouraged me to get back in the water regularly. This list isn't just for a laugh – it's a reminder 'you have the goods, now'.

'If Not You, Who?'

Liz Nable and I met when I joined her Media Masters Academy.

She begins our chat with a question. 'Raise your hand if you've ever doubted yourself,' she says with a knowing smile as I raise mine. 'Yes, I thought so.'

Liz's professional life began in journalism, where she spent 15 years working both in Australia and internationally. 'I thought if I kept my head down, worked hard, and didn't complain, someone would pick me,' she recalls. 'But I realised no-one was going to choose me to rise through the ranks – especially after I had kids. That seemed to push me further down the pecking order.'

That dawning was a turning point. 'I decided to choose myself.'

That decision led Liz to step outside her comfort zone and begin again as an entrepreneur. 'I realised that so many women, especially in mid-life, needed the same push to choose themselves. We're often overlooked, but we need to be the ones driving our own success stories. I help them create their own media and PR success without big agency fees.'

Her top tip for us when we feel uncertain? 'In practical terms, I would write a script for myself, practise in front of the mirror – then pick up the phone, organise a meeting, find an opportunity, and make clear my ask.' She laughs. 'Take it from me, this idea works!'

'Picking you means taking control,' Liz says. 'Stop waiting for someone else to promote you or tell you that you're good enough. Back yourself, all the way.'

It truly does – Media Masters Academy has garnered more than half a million dollars of organic media features and PR for her clients.

Liz Nable, founder of Media Masters Academy (and an entreprenuer). She empowers others – through coaching, speaking, step-by-step online workshops, and her 'Media Magnet' podcast – to take control of their narratives.

Realising More Shiny Things Will Not Serve You

A friend once joked that my next book should be about all the business ideas I had but never pursued. Instead, because I never felt 'ready' – I signed up for online courses (most I didn't finish) to teach me to be 'an expert'. The truth? We can become addicted to the pursuit of *something new* – chasing solutions, gurus, and quick fixes – shiny promises may seem attractive when looking for answers.

Mid-life can feel like standing at the edge of a candy store, grabbing whatever looks promising to fill a void. But all that glitters isn't gold. Sometimes, what we need isn't shiny or new – it's recognising the wisdom we've carried all along.

Upskilling with Intention

The pursuit of personal growth is essential, but so is discernment. Before signing up for a course, ask, *What am I hoping to gain? And more importantly, Do I already have the tools to take the next step?* Invest in yourself wisely. Whether it's a coach, a fitness trainer, or a supportive book club, choose the people and programs that align with your values. Learning is invigorating, but it should enhance your journey – not distract you from it.

Women's intuition is real. Listen to your inner compass steering you. The right path? There's a good chance it's not shiny.

WINTER POSSIBILITIES

Essential Steps from Winter – Feel Empowered

1. **Confidence and clarity reboot.** Rediscover your confidence by asking tough questions that guide your future.

   ### TRY THIS

   Take 10 minutes to list three values that matter most to you (e.g. health, freedom, family). Keep them visible.

2. **Financial foundations:** Align financial literacy with your mid-life goals.

   ### TRY THIS

   Spend two hours this weekend reviewing your finances. Identify one small improvement, like setting up automatic savings or cutting an expense.

3. **Simplifying your lifestyle.** Declutter your space and mind. Focus on what truly matters.

TRY THIS

Spend 30 minutes decluttering one room today. Remove five unused items. Schedule another 30-minute session later this week.

4. **Purpose rediscovered.** Reflect on what will bring joy and *raison d'être* to your next chapter.

TRY THIS

Write one sentence each night for a week about what will give you purpose. Use previous prompts for ideas.

5. **Begin to make your move.** Each action brings you closer to the life you envision.

TRY THIS

Set one small personal goal for tomorrow (for example, a 15-minute walk or organising a shelf). Do it first thing and build momentum daily.

SPRING
FEEL REINVIGORATED

Time to build momentum – a stronger mindset, a clearer path
forward – and a fresh perspective.

Practically speaking, Spring is the season to:

1. Action wellbeing and build firm healthy foundations.

2. Enjoy movement for optimum health benefits.

3. Learn how to eat for mid-life.

4. Build your physical strength.

5. Herald the arrival of your mid-life mojo and chic.

A Healthy Daily Practice Is Freeing (Not Boring)

When it comes to health and fitness, I've learned the hard way that there is no such thing as an overnight success. I wasn't born bursting with the thrill of exercise – with debilitating childhood asthma, Mum dragged me to swim club. As I outgrew asthma, I was diagnosed with thyroid cancer. When I finally found my strength, a 25-kg weight gain wouldn't shift. I tried it all, or so I thought. At the end of every week of effort, I'd be so discouraged I wasn't miles closer to my 'goals' I'd decide 'bugger it', and head back to the fridge and couch. Two steps forward, five back. I developed an eating disorder to boot (more on this later).

I finally realised the road to feeling better could be navigated by starting with small steps, consistently – no overarching 'goal' in mind, simply more kindness to myself and my broken body. Thirty years later, I know what works for me: trial and error, with one constant – perserverance. It's freeing.

Plan to Plan

The key to lasting wellbeing? Routine. Plan to plan, then stick to it long enough to feel better – and reassess when needed. No grand gestures, just daily actions that become as automatic as brushing your teeth.

In my experience, there is a greater chance of success in optimising wellbeing changes by eliminating options in the first instance. Yup. Apart from allowing for physical or dietary challenges, just follow the process to start.

Later, I will implore you to ENJOY your food – during changes, however, focus more on fuelling yourself to optimal satiety.

Do not go like a bull at a gate from day one; you will get bored, exhausted, and overwhelmed.

Continue to do all the digging you like on the wherefores – however, at some point you may as well begin to put your wellbeing at the top of your list of 'things to do' (after you are given a health clearance from a medical professional).

If you would like more research on how to overcome inconsistency in habit formation, read *The Habit Revolution* by Dr Gina Cleo.

Understanding the Not-So-Secret Secret of Feeling Better

Worth Repeating Often – Put Your Oxygen Mask on First

Diary Note…

As I reflect on my experiences, it was in prioritising my 'health narrative' that the 'rest' seemed to fall into place. For the most part, because I had energy to mull over my options and clarity to see possibilities, a sense of wellbeing descended and the fog lifted.

You get one body, period. Given it is such a precious commodity, you'd imagine we would treat it like gold dust. Surprisingly, we don't. Investigative tests, dental check-ups, skin scans – get pushed to the bottom of our 'to tackle' lists.

I've already pointed out how woefully down the hierarchical list of needs my own health investigation was. Honestly, I spent more time at the vet for our fluffy family members than I did at my GP. Amidst the needs of everyone else, I had forgone my health and wellbeing:

- My husband a shocking sleeper – I had become one.

- My son's athleticism requiring lots of fuel – I now ate more than I needed.

- I'd always exercised – but started to show up without fully showing up.

Due to the diagnosis of thyroid cancer in my twenties, I keep a handle on my blood work and iron levels because I'd thought that was the extent of my 'lack of energy' (no-one pointed out it could be peri-menopause). I schedule regular bone scans, boob and cervical tests, and dental check-ups. Otherwise, nada. I needed a baseline, where I sat on the scale of 'optimum health' versus 'get the woman to a hospital'.

Studies show your calendar age does not have to correlate with your 'body age'.

There are no guarantees in life, and I don't know about you, but if I can take charge of my health, sign me up.

But what should we be signing up to?

If we are designing an optimum mid-life together, health is where we need to begin. At the base level, I take it to mean your body is functioning at its prime for your life stage.

You will be going through your days with energy, you will be able to fight off illness, you will be physically strong, lithe, mentally alert, your sleep quality will be optimal, menopause systems might abate (or at the least be managed effectively).

Breakout

Fun fact: a blood test revealed I had the precursor to fatty liver – surprisingly, not alcohol-induced (a miracle after homeschooling two HSC teens). Many girlfriends had similar markers, possibly linked to hormonal shifts. Frozen shoulder, while not directly related to peri/menopause, is often linked by experts to these changes. The grapevine has been our go-to for so long, but finally (slowly), we are getting more data-driven answers.

TRY THIS

Spend a week focusing on any niggles or pain that might be so ingrained you barely notice. Take notes and talk to your doctor. Ask for a list of tests you might consider.

No-One Knows Your Body Better Than You

I was in my mid-twenties when I was diagnosed with thyroid cancer. I hadn't been feeling 'right' for a while – my lifestyle crawling the corporate ladder meant many nights 'entertaining' was the norm – so I put it down to 'I need a holiday'. Eventually, I booked a routine GP check-up – revealing a large lump in my neck (which I had completely missed due to busy, busy). Within a fortnight, I had been operated on twice and scheduled for radioactive treatment.

I had questions, so I asked my surgeon:

'Was this disease lifestyle related?'

'What could I do to increase my chances of a speedy recovery?'

'Would a special diet or yoga help?'

You may not be surprised that I was shushed, made to feel odd for even suggesting food and lifestyle might be 'part of the medicine' and that a mindful practice might help. Not his fault, really. Medical training didn't include such possibilities and society puts the medical profession on a pedestal. I ignored this and embarked on my own education. About five years after my treatment, a large-scale building project began as an adjunct to my surgeon's hospital and practice. The purpose? An integrated cancer treatment centre – the Chris O'Brien Lifehouse – providing holistic care for cancer patients.

I share my anecdote to urge you to do your research, find the best medical support team, listen to your body, and ask your questions. I am a slow learner – with my son's medical needs, and a perimenopause journey never linear, yet again, I failed to listen to my body, instead defaulting to 'advice' without my own thorough research.

TRY THIS

The List You Might Need with Dr Jean Hailes Clinic for Women's Health.

Good health can be taken in an instant. Some of you may feel sub-par. Know you are seen and applauded for your strength in the face of ill health.

jeanhailes.org.au/clinics

Jean Hailes for Women's Health is a national not-for-profit organisation dedicated to supporting Australian women's health through every stage of life.

As the official national digital gateway for women's health – recognised by the Australian Government – their website is full of valuable information and comprehensive free resources, including checklists to take to your own medical professional.

Hormones 101

Perimenopause is the time preceding menopause, 'how long is a piece of string' is how early it begins (for the sake of this conversation, let's say around mid-forties). Menopause occurs when you have not had a menstrual period for 12 months; fundamentally, it lasts for a day.

Just as our periods arrive at a no one-size-fits-all time, so too does perimenopause appear. Insidiously, it can creep in years before you are aware – as studies now show.

After turning 40, I began asking my GP for hormone testing related to menopause (this was 15 years ago and none of us, medico included, had a script for peri versus menopause). I felt something wasn't quite right, yet didn't have the narrative to ask questions. Well, apparently my hormones were A-okay – so I pegged sleepless nights and an overwhelming life situation.

Waves of internal combustion would fire up at random moments, fleeting, so I never remembered to question it. So, too, a sense of foreboding about everything – irrational chasing thoughts. Then panic attacks. One day I drove through the Sydney Harbour Tunnel. As daylight disappeared, the walls appeared to be closing in – I couldn't quite get my bearings to navigate the narrow lanes and speeding traffic. Within moments, my tongue became swollen, chest pounding so hard I thought I was having a heart attack, palms so slippery it was an effort to keep them on the steering wheel. My speed reduced to a crawl. A quick glance in the rear vision mirror was enough to get a sense of the mayhem I was beginning to cause. Ahead was a breakdown bay. I knew if I pulled over, that would be it – I would literally park and have to walk out. At the time, I put it down to the shock of the funeral I was about to attend. I felt shame that a self-professed 'in control' woman felt so 'out of control' – telling no one – resulting in 15 years circumventing our city, totally avoiding tunnels and freeways.

Listen to Dr Louise Newsome's podcast on why hormone testing may not always be the best path.

Research confirms depression and anxiety may increase in perimenopause.

Now the mid-life conversation has begun, we are armed with more menopause vernacular, and I understand my experiences related to a slew of physical and mental hormonal shifts – not a slide into madness.

TRY THIS

Adopt a 'trial and error' mindset, a willingness to do your own research – via experts and other women – to find the approach that works best for you. Closer to home, Dr Ginni Mansberg (more on her menopause program in Shelly Horton's chapter). In the US, Dr Erika Schwartz (Trinny Woodall has some interesting interviews on YouTube with Dr Erika), and aforementioned Dr Louise Newson, UK.

When Your Brain Decides to Play Hide and Seek

I've never particularly enjoyed walking into a room full of strangers (and yet, glutton for punishment, I chose a career that put me in this situation daily). I still don't love it, but I eventually learned to be comfortable with being uncomfortable. But I digress.

What I did bring to those awkward encounters was an uncanny ability to recall names on cue – always. It was a handy skill, one that has since decided to elude me in mid-life. Sometimes, it feels like my brain has taken an extended holiday without leaving a forwarding address.

Recently (so recent that I still feel the flush of embarrassment), I had a 'moment' – I forgot a good friend's name. Actually, it was worse than that; I thought she was someone else entirely! This friend has been in my orbit for 25 years. I know her well. I also know her name. Or at least, I used to.

At the beginning of this unpleasant tale, I was bumbling along at the gym, lost in thought, trying to recall the name of someone I met the day before (this trend could be concerning), when up popped my friend. At the gym for a work function (I know, I know – work dos used to be at the pub, but I must admit, I do prefer this work life version). The name I'd been trying to remember flew out of my mouth – 'Hello, (name of person she is definitely not).' The confusion on her face took a moment for me to register. Then the penny dropped … and even then, it took a minute for her actual name to slip into my mind.

Mild memory problems and general fogginess can be common in women navigating the roller coaster of peri/menopause – bear in mind, not every woman will experience these cognitive symptoms.

You see, oestrogen doesn't just keep our reproductive system humming; it's a key player in cognitive function. As our hormone levels drop, it can affect memory, concentration, and even our ability to multitask (which is practically a superpower for most women).

Remember, these mid-life brain blips don't define us. They're a reminder that our brains, like the rest of us, are going through changes. Optimum brain health as our cognitive ability declines with age is not my area of expertise, so I will not extend an opinion, simply raise ideas the experts in this field suggest we contemplate.

TRY THIS

- **Exercise.** Physical activity increases blood flow to the brain, which improves cognitive function. Even a brisk walk helps.

- **Mental stimulation.** Challenge your brain. Crossword puzzles, learning new languages, or even memorising your social media passwords keep it sharp.

- **Social connection.** Chatting with friends isn't just fun – it helps keep cognitive decline at bay.

- **Diet.** Omega-3-rich foods like salmon, leafy greens, and berries support brain function.

Kale is on the list. I know, sorry.

- **Sleep.** Aim for 7–9 hours a night. Sleep quality has a profound impact on memory and focus.

- **Stress management.** Chronic stress wreaks havoc on cognition. Explore meditation, yoga, or just scream into a pillow!

- **Hormonal support.** Speak with your GP about the role oestrogen plays in cognitive function – your needs may vary.

Insight: Shelly Horton – A Menopause Journey

MvT: 'Shelly, your mid-life trajectory has been anything but a 'straight line' – what do you wish you knew at the onset?'

Shelly: 'I've been a journalist for nearly 30 years. You can see me every week on national TV. I run two businesses: ShellShocked Media and Don't Sweat It.

At age 46, my ovaries started sputtering to a halt like a 1983 Datsun. It was *perimenopause,* but I didn't know that because I'd never heard that word in my life. I thought I knew about menopause. That's what happens to women in their sixties – they experience hot flushes and their periods stop, right?

Shelly Horton is a renowned journalist, national TV presenter, co-founder of Don't Sweat It, and member of the International Menopause Society.

'I didn't fall into that category. I was a fox and at the peak of my career.

So, when I started to feel anxious and depressed, I blamed stress. When I had hot flushes, I thought it was because I was overweight. I'd had 12 blissful years without a period thanks to my IUD – then suddenly, I had a full period and thought, *Jeez I'm really stressed.* The period was the only reason I saw a GP. Unfortunately, the GP didn't know about perimenopause either. I was sent for blood tests and an internal ultrasound. They came back showing no cancer, so I was sent on my way and told to meditate and consider taking up a hobby to relax.

'I reached the point where I was crying at least once a day for no reason (I wasn't sad). Then I lost my motivation to work. I would classify myself as a workaholic; not something to be proud of, but for me, not wanting to work felt as dramatic as having a broken leg. I would arrive at work and be able to rally for the 20 minutes I was on air debating a high-profile journalist. But I'd drive home in a flood of tears, chastising myself for sounding stupid on national TV. My confidence was so low I wanted to quit before they fired me. Then I had a period that lasted 62 days. So, after eight months of misery, it was my husband who convinced me to call on my friendship with Dr Ginni Mansberg and ask her to see me as a patient. Dr Ginni put me straight on HRT and a mild antidepressant. Within a month, I was back, baby! I was ME again. 'I look back at those nine months and don't recognise myself. I felt let down by the sisterhood for not talking openly about perimenopause. I felt upset that my first GP was oblivious. I felt outraged when I was sent to a psychologist for perimenopausal depression, and her first question was 'What's perimenopause?' I felt shocked that I thought about quitting when I was in my prime earning years. I felt robbed of nine months of my life. So, I've turned peri and menopause into my passion. And today we're here to let you know why Australian women, like me, need your help. I have been trying to educate myself about perimenopause ever since it hit me four years ago. I find I am still learning things every day. It affects 100 percent of women (who live long enough for their ovaries to start backfiring) and parts of the trans and non-binary community. Yet it's like yelling into the wind.'

Five Things That Shocked Me

1. **Lack of knowledge.** Menopause isn't discussed enough – at home, at work, or even in schools.

2. **Menopause lasts one day.** The lead-up is called perimenopause; after your period stops for 12 months, you are postmenopausal.

3. **Loneliness.** Symptoms can make you feel out of control and isolated.

4. **Dry eyes everywhere.** Not just 'downstairs'. Even eyes and skin dry out.

5. **Hot flushes vary.** Some women live at a permanently higher temperature – like me, always wanting the aircon on in winter.

So, education is key. We need to talk about it at work and at home. Our partners and family need to know about it so we are not struggling in silence. The time for silence is over.

Shelly Horton is a renowned journalist, national TV presenter, and co-founder of Don't Sweat It. Shelly champions women's health, including peri/menopause, through her courses and public speaking. She's also a corporate trainer, ambassador for several health organisations, and member of the International Menopause Society.

The Power of Doing Less

A Grown Up's Gap Year Diary Note…

It takes time at a wellness retreat in the Alps for me to shed a compulsion to 'fill the moments' with purpose. Catering to a clientele used to making too many decisions, the atmosphere is stripped back – everything you need and nothing more. The yoga room looks on to verdant grazing pastures and beyond to the extraordinary Alps. Claudine, resident meditation practitioner, asks us to focus on the light at their peak. 'Mountains are solid, steadfast,' she hums. I resolve to embrace a grounded base – try weightless rather than anchorless. My already light suitcase now feels burdensome. I want to feel fleet of foot. I ship half the contents home and vow to accumulate experiences rather than stuff.

Humans are a paradox – we seek community, but equally need to be alone in our thoughts to reconnect to life and self.

I am Dutch. We have the word *niksen* – the concept of doing nothing that has purpose or is productive. My versions vary slightly from the essence and include a long walk with no particular route. Moments of crystal-clear clarity come when I am swimming solo laps, hiking in nature, having a massage, and lying very still in bed just upon awakening. 'Doing nothing'. When was the last time you sat, doing nix – stopped the pull to be constantly seeking?

In yoga, during *savasana*, I've often mentally prepped (grocery lists, family members to call, gifts to buy, on and on). But with the benefits of slowing down evidenced in research – a reduction in anxiety, strengthening the body's immune responses, better able to manage stress and cope with life's curveballs, even slowing the ageing process – I've started to place more emphasis on achieving 'bugger all'.

Research suggests the primal need to seek and forage, once essential for survival, now fuels endless pursuit of stuff and validation.

A gift of mid-life is to take a moment to gaze into the distance and dream. My maternal grandmother was the 'queen of seemingly doing nothing' – sitting in her chair, facing the sun, watching the world outside go about its busy busy, eschewing any need to get worked up about, well, anything. She lived a healthy life until age 95 – I keep her image firmly in my sights if I resist *niksen*.

Quieting the need to 'do' takes practice – advice to follow from yogi Kate Kendall.

Loosen your grip on a need to 'go, go, go', then go and do nothing, on purpose.

Expert: Kate Kendall – Mid-Life Mindfulness

Sitting across from Kate Kendall, it's hard not to be drawn into her calm energy, which radiates despite the chaos she is about to describe. As we talk, I sense how motherhood, and being on the cusp of mid-life, has reshaped her.

Kate is co-founder and director of yoga at Flow Athletic in Sydney, Australia, and author and creator of the event Flow After Dark – Yoga Silent Disco.

'As I dance (and sometimes trip) into mid-life,' she begins, 'I've busily abandoned myself in family and business amidst a swill of hormones. Solitude has become the soothing balm that sedates my busy mind, radically reorganises my nervous system, and brings me home.' Her words carry a weight that comes from experience, and as I listen, I find myself nodding in agreement. The constant busyness – whether with family or work – can pull us all in a thousand directions, but Kate has discovered a way back to herself that is within the grasp of most of us.

She's not picky about where she finds this solitude. 'I can find it just about anywhere,' she says. 'A toilet cubicle, the beach, the cupboard, the bedroom, and – my personal favourite – my car. And if two minutes is all I have, I'll take it.' But for Kate, solitude isn't just a break. 'Quiet space enables me to hear what's most important, feel what needs feeling, and see what, in the cacophony, I could not see before.'

There's a beautiful simplicity in how she frames it. Growing up in the country, Kate says, solitude was woven into her life. 'It was easy then. I felt at one with the trees in the dark and quiet forest on our property. The sound of rain sprinkling on the pond felt like magic, and it's a memory I hold close to my heart.' Her voice softens as she reminisces, 'Then 'adulting' and things became complex – I began overpacking for this wild ride called life.'

Like many of us, Kate spent her twenties and thirties in a relentless pursuit to prove herself. 'The comparisons, the ferocity of wanting to feel special – that's what fuelled both an eating disorder and burnout. I'm still recuperating and may be for years.'

There's a pause, and I'm reminded of a Rumi quote: '*The quieter you become, the more you are able to hear.*' I share it with her, and she nods in agreement. It's that quiet, Kate explains, that she's learning to reclaim in mid-life. 'Far from enlightened,' she admits, 'my forties have provided an opportunity to wake the hell up and claim what sets me free.'

For Kate, this has meant embracing solitude without guilt. 'Taking time out wherever might feed my soul isn't indulgent – it's a pleasure that is in service to those I return home to and beyond. Mid-life is where it gets real. It's when I realised that I'm not going to be around forever. And if I were to write my eulogy tomorrow, I want to feel super inspired, as opposed to moderately glad.'

She continues, explaining how space away from work and the mundane is where she remembers who she is. 'It's where I remember that I love punk rock as much as I love the sound of my singing bowls. It's where I'm true and in service to that part of myself that's introverted and shy so I can go into a huge hall and guide 800 people through a yoga or breath experience. There's an authenticity here that's magnetic. When I'm living in that kind of alignment, my mind is quiet, I'm being true, I'm authentic, I'm whole. So, here's to creating many more moments of space and solitude. Ritual is in deep reverence to self – and if that ritual must take place in a toilet cubicle, so be it.'

I laugh, because we've read 'my spot' is the loo.

Kate Kendall is a leading yoga instructor with 20-plus years of experience, co-founder of Flow Athletic, and founder of innovative Flow After Dark – Yoga Silent Disco. Kate is dedicated to teaching mindfulness; she is the author of the book Life in Flow *and* The Space Between *course.*

Find Clarity in Nature

Vanessa Bell – sustainability advocate, Australian Merino wool champion, and intuitive – offers a unique perspective on nature's role in self-care and clarity.

Vanessa blends grounded, practical wisdom with spiritual insight, making her approach unique. She understands how confronting it can be to face patterns we've carried since childhood but believes that total acceptance brings clarity. 'Insights are anchored in the energy of the earth and its changing seasons,' she says. 'We're designed to live at a sensory level – exploring, touching, smelling, and tasting. Research shows immersion in nature not only lowers cortisol levels but also sharpens cognitive function, proving that our connection to the natural world is as essential as the air we breathe. When we overlay our senses with gratitude and intention, the way forward becomes clearer.'

Vanessa also hosts the podcast Fashion to Farmer, *a celebration of sustainable fashion.*

Vanessa reflects on how work and self-care were once intertwined: 'Like the stockmen on our properties, who move cattle on horseback, fully at ease with the rhythm of their surroundings', she says, 'the most direct path to clarity is through nature. At its core, self-care is about reconnecting with our intrinsic value – and yes', she adds, 'That means taking care of ourselves first. Clarity doesn't arrive through force; it sneaks in when you're present.'

Vanessa Bell is an eco-entrepreneur, sustainability advocate, and champion of Australian Merino wool (founder of a luxury knitwear business). Blending fashion and environmental commitment – in addition, Vanessa and her husband lead innovative mixed farming practices across three properties in New South Wales.

Breakout: Nature – Forest Bathing

My love of nature is ever-present, even at home, where palm frond wallpaper envelops my bedroom walls, bringing outdoors inside. It is glorious to wake to, yet nothing can replicate the true experience of *shinrin-yoku*, or forest bathing.

The rustling of leaves beneath feet, soft dappled sunlight filtering through the canopy of pines (crisp scent mingling with the earthy aroma of moss and damp soil) – there's something inherently soothing about being in a forest.

Shinrin-yoku, is a practice that originated in Japan in 1982, born out of a growing need to reconnect with nature amidst the pressures of modern, urban life. The term was coined as a response to the increasing stress and health issues that accompanied Japan's rapid industrialisation. By encouraging people to spend time in forests, *shinrin-yoku* offers a natural antidote to the hustle and bustle of city living.

The practice is simple – immerse yourself in the forest atmosphere and become enveloped in nature as you absorb the sights, sounds, and smells of the natural world.

Modern neuroscience reveals the combination of removal from routine, exposure to nature, and guided therapeutic practices creates optimal conditions for neuroplasticity – our brain's ability to forge new patterns.

You will find more information on my website – I am studying to be a certified forest bathing guide.

TRY THIS

Find a natural environment; focus on your breath, your senses (what can you hear, smell, see, touch) – if safe, consider going barefoot for a fully immersive and grounding experience. As a beginner, you might like to seek out guided experiences – look for well-reviewed and certified facilitators.

WEAR   PREPARE   ENVIRONMENT

Setting Up to Be a Sleep Slayer

If I could give my younger self one piece of advice, it would be this: **Sleep!** Not just those teenage Saturday morning sleep-ins, but real, uninterrupted, deep sleep. The delicious kind that makes your bones feel light, your mind clear, and your heart hopeful. These days? I'd trade (insert prized possession) for just one night of it.

The Chicken and the Egg: Stress vs. Sleep

- **The chicken.** Financial worries, hormonal shifts, relationship challenges – these will yank you from your slumber at 3 am. But decent sleep is necessary to handle those challenges. Without it, everything from decision-making to simply getting through the day feels like trudging through mud.

- **The egg.** Every healthy habit you cultivate – like eating nourishing food, exercising, and nurturing relationships – feeds into a positive sleep cycle.

In short, good sleep supports good life habits, and vice versa.

Leave it too long without prioritising rest, and you'll be caught in a loop of elevated cortisol.

And that is not good.

Symptoms of Sleep Deprivation:

- Body fat storage increases
- Irritability skyrockets
- Focus plummets
- Cravings for high-carb, high-fat foods rise
- Increased risk of type 2 diabetes, heart disease, and obesity

Sleep is the bedrock of optimal health. When it's solid, everything else follows.

Stanford's Science-Backed Sleep Practices

Research from Stanford University's 'sleep age' study offers straightforward practices to improve sleep quality.

1. **Stick to a schedule.** Go to bed and wake up at the same time daily, even on weekends.

2. **Morning light exposure.** Get outside within 20 minutes of waking. Natural light regulates your circadian rhythm.

3. **Create darkness at night**: Use blackout curtains or a sleep mask.

4. **Limit caffeine and alcohol.** Avoid both late in the day to keep sleep cycles intact.

5. **Mind your meals.** Finish eating at least two hours before bedtime.

Sleeping Apart: A Relationship Saver?

Consider adding **separate beds** to your sleep toolbox. Since our inner-city terrace does not have an abundance of spare bedrooms, my workaround was swapping our queen-sized bed for two king singles, Euro-style.

The result? Better sleep for both of us – sleeping apart might not be everyone's solution, but for us, it's been a quiet revolution.

Separate bedcovers might do the trick if you are not wanting separate beds.

Taking Note: Write It Down

At some point in my twenties – amid a swirl of missed deadlines, sleepless nights, and an overwhelming need for change – I became a **list maker**. It was an unexpected pivot; my parents were prolifically organised, which I took as perfect grounds to spend my youth rebelling against their structure.

Okay, technically, the university suggested I not return for a second year – one too many missed lectures.

Back then, my life was a perpetual mess. High school felt like a revolving door of forgotten assignments, lost bags, and panic-filled mornings. Things hit rock bottom when I dropped out of my law degree.

Fast-forward a few years, and I did the opposite – went full-throttle into routine and earned the affectionate title 'Miss Precise' from my family. Eventually, I found a sweet spot: *structured enough to stay on top of life but flexible enough to enjoy the unexpected.*

Why I Still Use a Moleskine (Yes, Handwriting Still Works)

For the past 35 years, everything I need to remember, from meetings to grocery lists, has lived in my trusty red Moleskine notebook.

If tech options work better for you, stick with them – this is not an anti-app manifesto.

There are a million sleek productivity apps out there, but for me, handwriting feels tangible. There's something deeply satisfying about crossing off a task with a pen. My notebook kept me sane during the chaos of early motherhood – those evening lists became a lifeline. Now, in mid-life, lists are mental declutter tools. They allow me to sleep better because I know everything I need to do is already accounted for.

With our hectic lifestyles, it's no wonder many of us struggle to 'sleep softly'. It's easy to feel overwhelmed and have your mind race just as your head hits the pillow. That's when lists become permission to rest.

Papa lives many time zones away – he wraps up our calls with 'Sleep softly, darling', his sentiment so calming.

TRY THIS

1. **Brain dump.** Spend 10 minutes writing down everything on your mind before bed. It's like emptying your mental pockets.

2. **Prioritise.** Pick the three most important tasks for tomorrow. Be realistic – progress beats perfection.

3. **Gratitude.** Jot down three things you're grateful for. It's a subtle but powerful shift in mindset before you sleep.

The Goal? Less Noise, More Calm

This isn't about squeezing more into your day; it's about finding space – both in your schedule and your mind. You might even stumble across that elusive extra hour you've been chasing.

Curious about the science of sleep? Dr Matt Walker's *Why We Sleep* book and podcast provide invaluable insights into better sleep.

The Wellness versus Wellbeing Malarkey

We've landed in a noisy world, saturated by wellness messaging. What follows is my investigation into how we might shift the needle – rediscover what **wellbeing** really means and carve space for it in our modern lives.

True efficacy doesn't need to shout. Do your homework before buying into wellness trends.

Diary Note…

… the smell earthy. Cows graze in the uniform fields off my balcony – bells tinkling in rhythm.

I head out on the hiking trail, winding through a small orchard. A pile of crimson apples at the gate, a sign inviting passers-by to help themselves. I instinctively polish the slightly misshapen fruit – I haven't done that for years and doubt my boys ever have – and that is the moment I am reminded that apples we buy in supermarkets don't need polishing; they are perfect globes, pre-shined and coated in goodness-knows-what to make them so. They also have no taste. This apple does, smelling of childhood memories, of good health, of flavour and nature and care.

I continue on the trail and, after a few hours of steady uphill climbing (and, yes, screaming legs), I am rewarded with a goat farm – nestled in the shadow of the mountains – complete with adjoining 'Heidi's Hut'. The goatherd is 12-year-old Edwin, with 17-year-old Johanna on cow-milking and cake-baking duty. I opt for Johanna's morning bake – a traditional pound cake heavy with plums, sweet and plump ('… and only a little sugar,' she tells me), with a side of goat's cheese (creamy and fresh). Finishing my respite as a group of hikers reach us – bidding farewell, I turn to wave and take in the vastness of the sky, the craggy peaks, and the utter sense of wellbeing.

It's completely perplexing how far we have strayed from what we know to be best for us (and the planet).

The Wellness Paradox

Wellness, of course, is a hot topic. At the time of writing, the global wellness industry is valued at several trillion dollars – a juggernaut promising transformation but often delivering confusion. You would think with the amount of money we pour into 'feeling better', we'd all be 'feeling better'. But are we? Allergies are on the rise, weight issues abound, and mental health challenges are more prevalent than ever.

Dan Buettner, who documented Blue Zone communities, said, 'Feeling better is the sum of a few small, easy choices.' It's a truth we tend to complicate. His research emphasises that longevity isn't found in gyms but in daily habits – walking to see a friend, gardening, or cooking together – integrating joy and movement into everyday life.

Like shepherds of Sardinia, who walk miles across rugged hills – not as scheduled exercise, but as movement woven into their daily lives.

We scroll through apps promising peace while missing the chance to take a deep breath. A friend told me she subscribed to five wellness apps, only to abandon them all, realising her best therapy was sitting quietly with her cat and morning coffee. I couldn't help but laugh – sometimes, what we need most is right under our noses.

Finding Middle Ground

What if the answer isn't about doing more, but about doing less?

We're bombarded by messages to *buy this, do this, take this*. It's overwhelming. But the irony is that slowing down – not ramping up – might bring us closer to what we need.

Author Gretchen Rubin suggests, 'Act the way you want to feel until you feel the way you want to act.' If we want to feel more grounded, we could start by acting grounded – turning off notifications, putting away devices, and engaging with what's in front of us.

And re-read Dr Danielle Einstein's tech chapter until it sinks in.

I'm not suggesting we quit our jobs to become Alpine goatherds. What I am proposing is a middle ground – a sweet spot where we combine the wisdom of the past with the convenience of the present.

Wellness, as it's sold to us, often chains us to unattainable ideals. Real wellbeing, however, lies in letting go – of expectations, trends, and the endless pursuit of betterment. We don't need the latest gadget or miracle superfood. It's about making informed choices – bona fide wellbeing, reclaimed from the wellness industrial complex.

State of Wellbeing

In relation to lifestyle, wellness can be seen as the means or actions taken to achieve a state of wellbeing. For example, you could practice yoga or follow a balanced diet (wellness activities) to achieve a state of satisfaction and happiness in life (wellbeing).

Here's what wellbeing looks like for me:

- Fit, lean, and strong (my preferred state)
- Rested and ready to wake with the sunrise
- Nutritionally balanced, ideally with minimal sugar
- Mentally clear – a tame monkey mind in flow
- Connected with my tribe – those I love, close and meaningful
- Purposeful and curious – excited to greet the day

This is my rhythm, but it's not universal. Your wellbeing might mean other things. The key is to find what works for you – whatever shape it takes – and build your life around it.

Of course, I have a family and a job; my days cannot be spent in the complete pursuit of wellness. A more integrated approach I've found sustainable. My conclusion is wellbeing can be found in the moments, wellness requires commitment to daily practices – the former the goal, but it cannot be achieved without a deliberate approach to the latter.

Wellbeing in a Noisy World

Growing up, my sisters and I enjoyed a childhood filled with clean air, outdoor pursuits, and simple pleasures. Sailing trips, long hikes, and orchard visits weren't luxuries – they were simply how we lived. I didn't fully appreciate those experiences at the time – the scent of fresh, ripe apples permeating the laundry for weeks after a trip to a local orchard, the seagulls squawking at the docks, and the salty tang of fresh fish from the port.

Mum kept mung beans sprouting on the kitchen sink, and every house we visited had a baking tin filled with treats – just enough to enjoy but not overindulge.

Years later, I tried to recreate that spirit for my boys – picnics in the park, dirty hands from climbing trees. But life gets noisy, doesn't it? Convenience creeps in. Pre-packaged health foods – promising everything, delivering little – begin to take over.

We don't need to return to baking every weekend (though nothing beats homemade), but we can learn to read ingredient lists and make intentional choices. Sometimes, the simplest things bring the greatest rewards.

TRY THIS

What small pleasures from your gen X childhood can you weave back into your life? A weekend farmers market? A family picnic? A game of tennis with friends?

Eating in Mid-Life Made Simple

Food Experiments, a Brief History

I know well how exhausting it is to feel a constant pull to excess. A disordered dance with 'what to eat' has long been a theme in my life. Perhaps yours, too? As a youngster, my appetite had no off switch – yet a busy body constantly on the move burned up most of the fuel. My teens saw bedlam: hormones, booze, '80s tuckshop food, and giant-sized missteps. A misguided notion that if I 'looked more like the girls in the magazines', all would be well in my world – thus I collided headfirst into a decade of bulimia. Food became both comfort and nemesis.

The real culprit? No single defining moment. I was loved (perhaps compliments came more often when I looked 'healthier') – although, when push came to shove, I suspect I probably read about someone losing weight this way and thought, *Cake and eat it? I'm in.*

Still, it was never about binge-eating junk. Even nutritious meals in vast quantities can be 'too much of a good thing'.

At some point, I have sipped from the well of most 'weight loss' and 'look better' programs. Some with limited success, others with dire consequences (one experiment resulted in near hospitalisation – as I became, ahem, 'backed up to the eyeballs'). Let's continue (a sample, the full list is long...), just for laughs:

Over a million Australians live with eating disorders, according to the Butterfly Foundation – seek help if you need it.

- Jenny Craig and Weight Watchers (WW did have merit as a kickstart)
- Maple syrup diet
- Thigh-reducing cream (Peter Foster's scam)
- 'French women don't get fat'
- Keto (a Euro-trip on protein alone; I still weep for the shunned baguettes)

All 'failures' led to a low-grade buzz of discontent. You know the trope:

- When I am thinner, I will …
- When I have less cellulite, I will …

Without unlimited time and funds, and giving enough of a crap, it's a rubbish mountain to scale. Whose standards do we seek to uphold? The answer should be: *ours.*

Hello, Nutritional Sanity

My 'line in the sand' moment? Pregnancy. Nothing like growing a human to shift your perspective – wanting to lead by example for my sons led me to qualify as a nutritionist. Perhaps a better one because of my own tangled history with food, not in spite of it. Two decades later, when perimenopause and circumstances wreaked havoc, I had the tools to adapt. It's a reminder that how we *perceive* food matters just as much as what we eat. A Yale study found that participants who believed they were drinking an indulgent milkshake experienced a greater reduction in hunger

Bombarded by clever marketers, 'lose weight fast' messaging is insidious. My 'food experiments' were laughable, and I know this stuff.

172

hormones than those who thought it was a healthy one – both groups consuming the same shake. Finding your way to intuitive eating is key. Forget 'one-size-fits-all' diets. Intuitive eating means listening to your body's signals – something we knew how to do before marketers told us otherwise. It's not a free pass to eat cake at every whim; it's learning to tune out the noise. Some days you'll crave veggies, other days that piece of cake. Think of it as a lifelong friendship with food – give and take, trust and forgiveness. It takes practice, but eventually you will reconnect with your natural hunger and fullness cues, and then you can drop your shoulders, let out a sigh of relief – leave the noise behind and enjoy food.

Breakout

The sum of us is not our size. Our generation has lived the gamut of 'body shaming' commentary, including 'nothing tastes as good as thin feels' – all with little regard for the fact that *none of us are the same*. We don't look the same, we won't be the same stature, our muscle mass will differ, as will our skeletal frame, and so too what we weigh. I've avoided escalating *weight* in our conversation – yet it is what I am asked most often: *How do I lose weight?*

The answer? If we feel better about our lot in general, what to eat may well end up way down the list of aggravations. Rather than agonising over which 'weight wagon' to hitch to, you'll find yourself naturally enjoying food in just the right amounts. The *shoulds* will fall away as you tune into what your body needs. Enjoying food – minus the confusion – will re-surface.

If 'reduction' for health is on your agenda, seek support if you are struggling.

When hormones alter metabolism, it can feel all too hard – but it is not impossible to make positive lifestyle changes. In my experience, as I began to treat myself like a project and took a step back to view myself in the abstract, it became easier to make sensible decisions for lasting, more healthful outcomes. At some point, I decided that the overarching theme shouldn't be how I looked but rather ensuring future me is strong, nimble, and in long-lasting good health.

There's enough on our plate without adding 'population'-designed protocols – so get professional advice for your body.

Food Is Fuel

Diary Note …

When I visit family in Europe, weekend lunch might stretch for hours, no-one rushing to clear the table and dessert – thinly sliced fruit – savoured with a few 'petite tartes'. Here, meals aren't fuel or enemy, but a ritual of connection. It makes me wonder: when did our relationship with food become so transactional, measured in macros and calories?

Eating well fuels you to feel energised, balance hormones, support bone and muscle health, and keep your mind sharp. Nutrition basics are a journey, not a destination. You deserve to enjoy food without guilt or anxiety. The goal is to feel better (looking better, if desired, will be a bonus). Be patient; celebrate small victories.

Seek professional advice if this is your first 'better nutrition' journey.

With this caveat in place:

- Take advice from good sources and make your routine your own.
- Continue the great things you do – ditch what no longer serves you.
- Form a 'solid nutrition' base.

I cleaned up my nutrition not by following some arbitrary list of good and bad foods but instead by looking for beneficial additions to my nutrition lifestyle. Guides, not chains; a framework for freedom, giving you the confidence to make choices without the need for constant willpower battles – creating a sustainable approach. I enjoy food, of course I do. But foremost is how to eat to feel better. To that end, ever mindful:

- It is not your imagination, changes in hormones (specifically oestrogen) do cause more fat to be stored around your midsection. Adopting healthy nutritional changes can produce positive results.

- All other factors being optimal (sleep, hormones, muscle mass) – understand the balance of your energy equation. The old adage 'calories in vs calories out' oversimplifies things – a professional can explain the optimal way forward for your body.

- Be wary of wild claims and promises of quick solutions.

A recent study by Zoe Health shows dietary changes may decrease certain symptoms in peri/menopause by up to 37%.

The end.

Except it's not, is it?

What Suits Me Will Not Likely Suit You

The second question is: what do I do every day for wellbeing? Reading between the lines, the question really boils down to, 'What exactly do I eat?' I tend to deflect as we come with completely unique circumstances – I encourage 'what serves you best, is what serves you best'.

We know mid-life is another one of life's transitions – it stands to reason that 'what always worked' may no longer. When our hormones are swinging, our sleep broken, our muscle mass diminishing, our bone density reducing, our hair thinning, our eyesight failing, our joints aching, our gut health suffering, our waistlines expanding, excitement about sex a distant memory … need I go on … it might feel like we should throw up our hands and admit defeat. Including working out which foods are best for longevity in health (and in forms we enjoy).

Please don't give up. You are at the reins of this circus pony; step up and take charge, for your health's sake. Finding your nutrition nirvana will pay dividends – in every aspect of life. I am proof of this, as are many other women. It's worth repeating that what works wonders for your best friend might not do the same for you, even when you have the same genetics; my time-restricted eating, mostly plant-based, minimal-carbohydrate fuel is superb for me, but my younger sister requires more carbs and more frequent meals.

Additionally, what suits today will require tweaking as I age (incorporating more protein, fibre, and perhaps supplements). The point is this: do your research. Experiment. Make a plan. Stick to it for the most part while it works. Refine it when it doesn't.

Having already acknowledged it is no easy ask – ultimately, what you eat is on your shoulders.

Decide to take personal responsibility for your health and nutritional intake.

While relearning nutrition basics, an initial approach of viewing food as 'simply fuel' has helped many clients take pressure off themselves. It doesn't detract from the pleasure of a great meal but allows space from constant decision fatigue:

Am I hungry, bored?

Is this too much, too little?

Which version of x, y, z is better?

Do not take this responsibility lightly. We are intelligent women; we know it shouldn't be this hard. Nutrition is my bag; even so, I remain a perpetual student. Tracking patterns (sometimes with a glucose monitor) gave me new clarity – it turns out, my 'perfect breakfast' of oats wasn't perfect for me after all. Add blueberries, and the so-called superfood became a mid-morning crash waiting to happen. Addressing the needs of the individual, rather than a collective approach, for the win.

Where to Start: The Art of Real Food

Begin with the simplicity of author Michael Pollan's advice: 'Eat food, not too much, mostly plants.' A great place to start. Eating real food, mindfully and in moderation, allows you to reconnect with your body's natural signals and enjoy food without guilt.

Hippocrates had the right idea 2,000 years ago: 'Let food be thy medicine.'

Pollan's philosophy aligns with sustainable eating habits. It's not about chasing fads but forming a healthy relationship with food that can evolve over time. Think of it as a framework, not a prescription:

- Eat real food – ingredients you recognise, as close to their natural state as possible.
- Enjoy your meals mindfully – take time to savour, share, and connect.
- Stay curious – experiment with what works for you and adapt as needed.

Breakout: Gut Feeling

The gut-brain connection – once fringe theory, now well-established – reminds us how deeply intertwined mental and physical wellbeing are. With about 95% of serotonin produced in the gut, it's no wonder digestive health shapes not just what we eat, but how we feel.

Through my own journey with thyroid cancer, perimenopause, and gut issues, I learned to listen closely to what my body needs – and what it no longer tolerates. For me, this meant cutting out onions, garlic, and wine, as even a sip left me bloated and uncomfortable. The body sends messages constantly; our job is to listen.

Start with bloodwork before leaping into 'supplements'. Individual solutions always trump the one-size-fits-all advice – consult a professional for 'best for you'.

The Wisdom My Grandmothers Knew (and Probably Yours, Too)

When I feel confused about 'which path to follow', I remember both grandmothers lived well into their nineties, enjoying lifestyles that would put many modern wellness trends to shame. Meals were about community and nourishment, not calorie-counting or macros. They revolved around family rituals, gardens, and real food from local farmers – bottled plums and homemade pickles appearing long after one had passed. They consumed alcohol in moderation – a small whisky or local wine, sipped as part of a convivial gathering.

Grandma's minestrone simmered on the stovetop all winter, replenished with beans and fresh vegetables. She never once uttered the word 'wellness' – she simply lived well. My Belgian

Oma, on the other hand, delighted in 'petite tarte' and *frites* with mayonnaise, but never in excess – again, balance and pleasure.

Snacks were simple – fruit, cheese, or a handful of nuts. They lived with purpose and rhythm, without a diet manual or wellness app.

Breakout

And yet, they weren't immune to misguided advice. Grandma smoked like a chimney – handed her first cigarette as a teen under the guise of 'stress relief' during the war, a doctor-endorsed health tip of the time.

TRY THIS

1. Consider reading Pollan's *In Defence of Food* to explore simple, sustainable eating habits.

2. For one week, jot down what you eat and how you feel – energy, digestion, mood. Notice patterns and adjust accordingly – use this insight to refine your eating habits.

This is your friendly reminder to research even the best advice – it's not gospel just because it's given with authority.

3. You could also sign up for a reputable nutrition course to boost your knowledge for informed, empowered choices. While you won't become an expert overnight, you will be more confident making better food choices.

How to Actually Do Food Prep

'But wait,' you say, 'I don't even have time to sit, let alone feed myself!'

Maybe – except if you don't eat nutritious meals, you will, quite literally, fall down.

The next statement puts me out on a limb – I am okay with this and remain firm on the topic. You do need to feed yourself well, this involves knowing how to cook. It may not be an activity you enjoy, and that's neither here nor there. You also may be 'over' producing dinners on tap for all and sundry.

My three-degree-holding, mathematical husband refused to 'learn to cook', expressing he 'lacked an affinity' with 'throwing ingredients together'. Preparing a meal for him meant methodically following a recipe, which seemed like hard work. It took me leaving him for eight months for his hand to be forced. He now delights in taking our Sunday evening meals to exciting heights, inviting our boys' friends to join in.

As with everything in life, it requires a little planning, a bit of common sense, and a willingness to give it a go. YOU can cook!

I now seldom find pleasure in preparing day-to-day meals. For these, I stick to the rudimentary and easy to produce for the greatest nutritional punch.

Try doing it for 20 years – equating to a loose estimation of 14,560 meals!

'Clapping hands'.

Breakout:

Important to Note … The Booze Chronicles

This isn't meant to critique my parents. A different outcome if I'd been 'sheltered'? Unlikely. One sister barely drank – same exposure, different story.

That nothing truly terrible befell me is sheer luck.

A disastrous choice mid-perimenopause: alcohol worsened hot flushes and sleepless nights.

Long-lived populations enjoy daily moderate, social alcohol.

I was in my early teens when I got drunk for the first time – horrifying, but not necessarily an anomaly in a Gen X childhood. Alcohol casually permeated our lives in ways that seem startling now. My route to booze may have been extreme, though a chat with friends suggests it wasn't far off.

The cultural obsession with alcohol created the perfect storm for someone like me – adventure-seeking, desperate to fit in, inwardly shy but with a loud front. My teens and twenties were marked by memories, viewed through the bottom of a glass. After a cancer diagnosis in my twenties, I quit cold turkey. Since then, there have been years where drinking played a bigger role than others – COVID brought on daily gin o'clock. Some friends will recall occasions watching me slide down a wall, or shamefully, a son required to escort me home.

Now, there's a growing conversation around being 'sober curious'. Many Gen Zers are rejecting the booze-soaked culture, opting for clarity. Alcohol's impact on our bodies and minds is well-documented, but whether to drink or not is personal. A social drink with a meal remains one of life's joys for many communities However, no-one should feel 'less than' for abstaining. During sober periods, I was labelled 'boring' and often resorted to pretending I had an alcoholic drink in hand.

These days, I often decline as I'm leaning into adventures I'll actually remember and finding healthier ways to feel brave. If alcohol isn't serving you, and you're struggling, seek professional help.

A gin martini remains a pleasure – an 'occasion' rather than a 'must have'.

Putting It Together

Armed with the basics of mid-life nutrition, you're ready to put theory into practice. Remember when we talked about treating yourself as a project? This is where that mindset really pays off. As Mel Robbins, author and motivational speaker, says, 'You  are one decision away from a totally different life.' In the context of our nutrition, each meal is a decision point – a chance to nourish ourselves better. Data shows people who plan their meals are more likely to have a healthier diet and lower obesity rates. It's time to become the project manager of your own wellbeing. Ready to craft your personal nutrition roadmap?

That Daily Food Plan You Mentioned?

We've explored the importance of intuitive eating and finding a personalised approach to nourishment. What follows is practical principles – this isn't a one-size-fits-all solution, so I am not giving you an 'eat this' chart. Instead, I encourage you to take the time to experiment with an eating plan you can sustain for life.

Day Five 'Gap Year' Diary...

I thought that, once released from the shackles of routine, I'd aim for 'fly, flop, and plough through the buffet' – instead, I'm sticking to my well-trod routine – wake, lie quietly for a moment and savour the good grace of a cosy bed, contemplating whether I feel good or not (jet lag AND hormones make a restful night's slumber a lottery). Either way, throw back the covers and get on with getting on. Shower, cold blast, off for a walk with a podcast, some form of strength training, protein-fuelled late breaky. The only discomfort is when I DON'T do – feeling as energised as I can is no easy feat these days.

In terms of how I nourish myself, I enjoy lots of unpredictability in life. Conversely, my day-to-day regime is mundane and requires zero effort to execute – I just do it. Although I could do better in some areas, principally it works. Perhaps all this makes you think, *Jeepers, I'll end up the most boring person in the room.* You won't! You will have more energy and pave a path to positivity and good health, while releasing anything that may be diminishing your wellness.

The nutrients in the food you eat determine how you thrive, especially as your body changes. Here's the short version: eat nutrient-dense foods of the highest quality, in quantities your body needs, relative to your movement. Aim to focus on predominantly plant-based foods, minimally processed, and a limited intake of animal products (if this works for you).

Making SPACE for the Joy of Eating

My regime 'methods', curated over decades, working with women, researching, and a hefty dose of common sense. *Bon appétit!*

Shop

Shop the perimeter of the supermarket. Fresh, wholesome foods are found where they're most likely to spoil. Stick to the produce, dairy, and meat sections – this is where the good stuff lives. Leave the middle aisles for household supplies and chocolate emergencies.

Long shelf life? Leave it on the shelf. If it can't spoil, should you even eat it? Real food doesn't last forever, but it nourishes you properly. The exception? Frozen fruits, veggies, and tinned legumes – convenience is your friend.

Replace processed snacks with real food. Ditch the packets and replace processed snacks with the real deal. Fruit, cheese, or nuts will satisfy your cravings and keep you away from unpronounceable ingredients.

Choose nutrient-dense foods. Opt for foods that pack a nutritional punch. Dark leafy greens, berries, fatty fish, and whole grains are excellent choices. These foods provide essential vitamins, minerals, and antioxidants that support overall health and can help manage mid-life changes.

Plan

Pre-plan your meals. Having a daily plan eliminates the 'I had nothing, so I grabbed something random' scenario. A little forethought goes a long way – especially when healthy eating is the goal.

Breakout

I find extensive food prep too boring. Two days of meals in advance is about right – the same base meal with different vegetables for variety.

Plan a weekly seasonal eating day. Hit up your local farmers' market or the seasonal produce section and plan a day of meals around what's fresh. You'll feel like a local hero supporting small growers, and your body will enjoy the feast.

More tips in my eCookBook – The Only Five Recipes You Need in This Lifetime (unless you love to be in the kitchen).

Adopt These Hints

Hydration and mindful eating. Drink enough: hunger and thirst are often confused. Drink water before meals and throughout the day. Herbal teas are great, too; my favourites are spiced with cinnamon, cardamom, or liquorice. They're like a hug in a mug.

Question your hunger. Before reaching for a snack, ask yourself if you're really hungry. If you wouldn't eat an apple, you probably aren't. It's about mindful eating, not mindless munching.

Satiated, not stuffed. Enjoy your food but know when to stop. Think 'satisfied', not 'stuffed'. *Hara hachi bu*, or eating until 80% full, is a great habit to develop. If you find yourself reaching for extra snacks, 'brush your teeth' – minty breath a great deterrent to mindless nibbling.

Regular check-ins and adjustment. Take stock regularly. Every couple of months, check in on your habits. Track your food, mood, sleep, and movement for five days. It's like hitting the refresh button, making sure nothing's creeping in unnoticed.

Clothes vs. scales. Scales can be misleading. But when your favourite jeans start to feel snug, take it as a nudge – not a punishment. Remember, weight fluctuates, but your wardrobe will always give you the truth.

Unless you alter your wardrobe sizing.

Try a detox. I like a whole-food-based detox every six months – viewed as a reset or a 'kick start' approach. Seeing results will spur you on! Look for a program that fits your lifestyle and has positive reviews.

Lifestyle habits. Tech-free time: dedicate one evening a week to a tech-free gathering. Turn off the screens and have a proper conversation with friends or family. Food and connection – two of life's greatest joys.

Create actions, not emotions. Remember the chat above on 'creating the actions of the person you want to be' – keep the emotion out of food and follow a plan. Seeing results when you put in effort is exciting. Decide on a lane (a program, tracking food, and so on) and stick to it.

Cook

Learn to cook quick, easy, fresh meals. My rule of thumb: 20 minutes from fridge to table. That's faster (and cheaper) than ordering takeout, and you know exactly what's going into your food. Simple doesn't mean boring.

Takeaway for treats. Sure, cooking is ideal, but don't fear the occasional treat. Just be picky about where you order from. It's about balance, not restriction, so let the takeaway be a treat, not a habit.

Eat

Put protein in the picture (and full-fat, too). These powerhouses keep you satisfied and your energy levels steady. No-one ever regretted a slice of salmon or a dollop of full-fat yoghurt.

Size up your sizing. If I have overindulged, I might eat meals for the next few days on a side plate, and perhaps use chopsticks – this helps me to reset to mindful eating.

Bye-bye buffet. Serve individual portion meals – putting the remainder away for another meal – rather than large serving platters in the middle of the table making 'seconds' too easy.

Let's get together. Gather around the table with friends or family and enjoy the food, the conversation, and the connection.

Enjoy food without guilt. Eat joyfully. A meal should feed the body and the spirit; eat well and savour each bite.

Seek Out Help If You Need To

Confused? Or want a tailored meal plan? Look for a registered nutritionist or dietician with an excellent track record. 'Socials' are not the place to take 'expert' advice unless qualifications apply to the mouthpiece. Try:

– Dieticians Australia

– The Nutrition Society of Australia

– Australian Traditional Medicine Society

Do your research and look for testimonials from other women.

As you implement these strategies, pay attention to how your body responds and don't hesitate to make adjustments along the way. Your mid-life journey is unique, and your nutrition plan should be too.

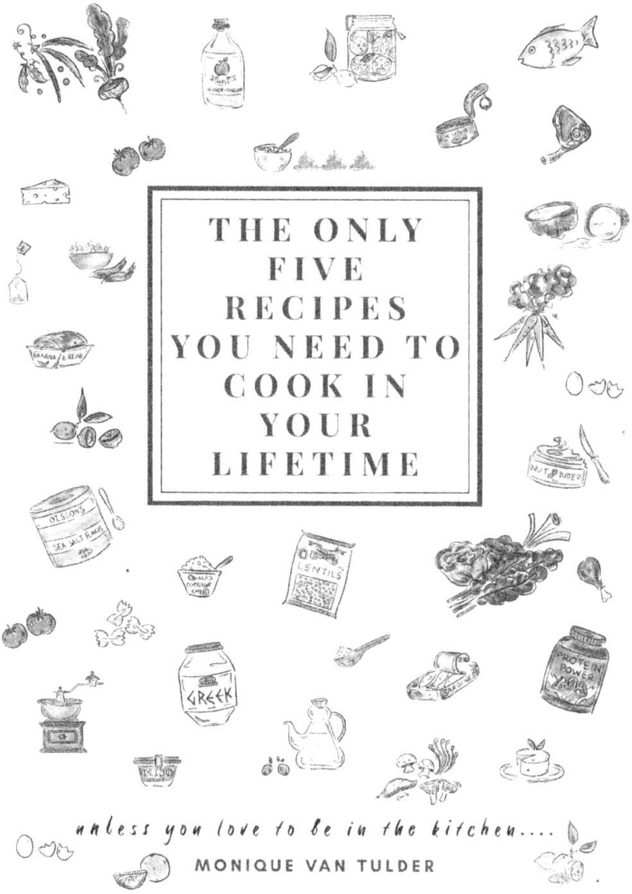

THE ONLY FIVE RECIPES YOU NEED TO COOK IN YOUR LIFETIME

unless you love to be in the kitchen....

MONIQUE VAN TULDER

SCAN HERE

With This Recipe, You Have Breakfast, Lunch, and Dinner

This meal can be on your plate quicker than the time it takes home delivery to arrive. Promise!

Cheaper, too – as my youngest discovered after having to pay me back for the expensive delivery meals he ordered.

Substantial Omelette

serves 1 (easily adjusted to feed more)

Splodge of olive oil

1 whole egg (extra if you prefer a more substantial meal)

2 egg whites

Whisk eggs together with a fork until well combined. Add olive oil to a small frying pan, heat gently, add eggs. Depending on size of pan to volume of egg, you may need to gently lift the edges to allow uncooked egg on top to reach the heat. When cooked through, turn off heat. Flip omelette in half. Serve with sea salt and pepper to taste.

Breakfast Option

Add baby spinach and mushrooms to the pan, wilt slightly before adding egg mixture. Turn to low and cook until egg cooked through.

Lunch Option

Handful of torn rocket and fresh herbs

2 tablespoons of cottage cheese

Sauerkraut/pickles, lemon wedge

As for breakfast, with the addition of cottage cheese on top. Place under griller for final few minutes to brown cottage cheese. Sprinkle sea salt. Serve with fermented sides and lemon wedge. Add extra protein as a side dish.

Dinner Option

1 tablespoon Persian feta,

2 chunks parmesan cheese

Chopped parsley

Smoked salmon (or home-poached if you have the energy)

Cook as per lunch. Sprinkle with parsley, serve smoked salmon on the side, and consider the addition of a glass of great wine.

Moving in Mid-Life – a Manifesto

Move; It Feels Good

Go and put on your BEST fancy workout gear – and if your stuff is daggy and saggy, bin it. Start this chapter fresh, motivated, and ready to lace up those trainers. Movement is a kind of rebellion in mid-life. It's shaking off the inertia that accumulates when life, responsibilities, and expectations weigh you down.

Movement is freedom. It increases your energy levels, gets your blood flowing, aids your 'best self' – for optimum health and longevity.

A leading cause of requiring assisted living later in life is not having enough fitness to perform basic physical movements.

Modern life encourages us to be physically lazy. How bizarre is it that we throw our washing in the dryer only to rush to the gym and do arm raises and squats – basically the same movements our grannies did hanging laundry? Movement isn't just about going to the gym. Healthy populations walk – a lot. They don't call it exercise; they call it living. More exertion, everywhere, all the time.

Take the stairs, walk more, take public transport, shop locally, hang washing on the line, start a veggie garden.

Breakout

A study followed 25,000 participants, aged 42 to 78, for eight years, measuring the positive effect of incidental exercise (you know, those 'boring' household chores). Researchers noted huffing and puffing for just 1–3 minutes during continuous movement could significantly decrease cardiac events. Bottom line? Every bit of movement counts.

Keep Moving

I've thrown myself off cranes to bungee jump, paraglided off mountains, and schussed down snowy slopes. But let's be clear – I have friends who make my escapades look like casual Sunday strolls in comparison. The point is, do something you can sustain, something that brings a smile to your face, gets your blood pumping, unblocks your mind, and unfurls your limbs.

When the monotony of the same walking route dulls your enthusiasm, try signing up for an event. A fun run, group swim, or even a gym challenge – giving your efforts a purpose can make all the difference.

In my early thirties, life was a whirlwind of work travel, early mornings, and late client dinners – not exactly a recipe for exercise enthusiasm. Sure, I moved every day, but I was just going through the motions. I needed a goal big enough to break me out of the rut, so I signed up for the Sydney Marathon – 42.195 kms of sheer grit.

Let's establish – I am not a runner. Not then, not now. But I was determined to feel better. Training was a riot of 5 am Saturday alarms and 'leisurely' four-hour runs in the dead of winter. We ran the coastline in pitch black, icy headwinds sometimes slowing us to a snail's pace, giving me plenty of time to question my sanity. For the first month, I practically crawled up hills that felt like Everest, while my then-boyfriend (now hubby) sang 'American Pie' to distract me from my screaming calves and trembling hamstrings.

This is when I knew he was a keeper, despite swearing I'd leave him if he made me talk whilst training.

I almost didn't make it to the start line. My fear nearly talked me into a cosy brunch instead. But I showed up. And I ran – for nearly five hours. My race time was so slow I was almost disqualified – but bloody hell, I did it. That memory and those endorphins still kick me out of bed whenever I waver.

As we age, we're not just stagnating – we're sliding backwards unless we consistently challenge our bodies. Movement isn't just about getting fit or shedding weight – it's a celebration of life.

Breakout

Find Your People to Move With

Connection doesn't just happen – it's a practice, an active choice. My local gym in Airlie Beach, North Queensland, illustrates this perfectly: women from every decade come together for weekly classes, lingering afterwards for coffee and conversation. It's more than just fitness; it's a community. A beautiful support network that extends well beyond the gym walls – as Fitness Venue gym founder Kerrin Andrew experienced herself. After a serious accident and ensuing hip replacement, she returned to teaching strength and yoga classes in record time. I ask what she credited her speedy recovery to. 'Decades of commitment to my physical fitness, a mindfulness practice – and our community,' she says. Her doctor echoed this. Kerrin's journey – much like the essence of *A Grown Up's Gap Year* – is a reminder: lay the groundwork now, and you'll be better prepared for life's inevitable curveballs.

If you're ever in Airlie Beach, come join us – it's as much about community as it is about strength.

Every run, every stretch is a reminder: 'I am here, and I am capable.' So, here's my mid-life movement manifesto: Move because you can. Move because it feels good. Move because your body is a gift, not a burden. And most importantly, move because you deserve to feel amazing in your own skin.

TRY THIS

1. Challenge yourself to incorporate more incidental movement into your daily routine. Incorporate exercise 'snacks' throughout your day – seize any opportunity to move.

An inexpensive fitness tracker is a quick way to keep an eye on progress.

2. Plan a walking meeting with a friend or colleague instead of sitting at a café.

3. Investigate the merits of a standing desk. Regular sitting a 'silent killer'; data links it to higher risks for health problems, particularly cardiovascular disease.

Understanding Why Getting Strong Makes Sense

I make it a priority to be strong – really, really strong. I want to be ready to face any adventure that might come my way. I know you do, too.

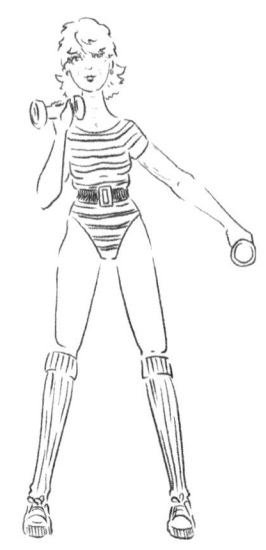

Building strength and muscle tone should be part of your non-negotiable wellbeing routine. Adventure aside, a key motivator is a recurring fear: falling off the loo in older age and being unable to gather myself upright – the boys having to hoist me and my knickers up. A spectacle I keep front of mind if I can't be bothered with my daily practice.

TRY THIS

The ability to get yourself down (and up) from the ground (without using your hands) is a predictor of longevity.

How did you go?

Not easy, is it?

After 30, muscle mass decreases by 3–8% per decade, with a more noticeable decline after 60.

Muscle strength is imperative for keeping us mobile in mid-life. This relates to both muscular strength – the ability of your muscles to exert force, allowing us to lift objects – and muscular power – the ability of your muscles to work efficiently, such as when climbing stairs. Strength training reduces muscle loss (sarcopenia) and can speed up your metabolism.

I can't see a downside, so I will let Sally-Ann Cowen take you through your paces in the next chapter.

Expert: Sally-Ann Cowen – Start Getting Strong

The first thing you notice about Sally-Ann Cowen is the ease with which she talks about strength – both physical and mental – as if they're two sides of the same coin. 'Strength training has been a part of my life since I was 14,' she tells me, with the quiet confidence of someone who's lived what she preaches. 'This means that I have been lifting weights consistently for 24 years.'

Sally originally set out to study medicine, but strength training rewrote the script for her career. 'I pivoted to exercise sports science and dietetics,' she explains, 'because I wanted to be part of the health promotion and ill-health prevention movement. I wanted to effect change.' Her passion isn't just about physical fitness – it's about empowering people, especially women, to discover their strength in every sense of the word.

When I ask what advice she has for mid-life women like us who are ready to get strong, Sally's enthusiasm is palpable. 'I've worked with women from 13 to 83 years old. Watching their transformation has been beautiful – seeing not only their muscles grow, but also their self-confidence, self-worth, and resilience.' She adds, 'It's extraordinary how resistance training can improve not just your body but your mindset and relationships too.'

Sally doesn't mince words when it comes to the importance of strength training. 'Research continues to prove that resistance training provides the greatest health benefits across all life stages,' she says. 'There are many types of training, and they all have their merits, but nothing compares to resistance training.'

The impressive range of benefits include (but are not limited to):

1. Faster metabolism
2. Reduced body fat
3. Increased strength
4. Improved mental health, including improving the effects of anxiety and depression, and slowing and halting the effects of Alzheimer's and dementia
5. Increased bone density
6. Balanced hormones
7. Increased testosterone
8. Increased growth hormone
9. Improved mobility and flexibility
10. Increased strength in tendons, ligaments and joints
11. Improved coordination
12. Anti-ageing effects
13. Healthy sex drive
14. Less pain
15. Less injury
16. Increased insulin sensitivity and carbohydrate metabolism
17. Reduced risk of heart disease
18. Improved blood pressure
19. Improved cholesterol
20. Reduced visceral fat
21. Better sleep

To make it practical, Sally breaks down her sessions using seven primal movement patterns – moves that mirror the things we do every day without thinking. She explains:

 **Squat.** 'Think sitting on the toilet.'

Lunge. 'That's walking.'

 **Hip hinge.** 'Bending to pick something up.'

Push. 'Ever lift overhead luggage?'

 **Pull.** 'Opening a door.'

 **Rotation.** 'Turning back in the car to check on the kids – or waving at your fabulous friend driving by.'

Plank. 'So you don't get knocked over when someone bumps into you.'

We laugh together at the thought of turning everyday moments into mini-strength sessions. But Sally is emphatic: 'It's about showing up for yourself and feeling capable, inside and out.'

Sally-Ann Cowen is a fitness and wellness expert with extensive university degrees and qualifications in exercise science, nutrition, integrative health and resistance training. She takes a holistic approach to health, helping clients build physical and mental strength. Sally's greatest joy comes from witnessing her clients' transformations from the inside out.

TRY THIS

Start with one day a week of strength training and slowly progress up to two or three days per week. And if you're a beginner, seek help and guidance from a fitness professional – and eat more protein! Other practices to incorporate to help maximise the benefits of strength sessions include:

- Foam rolling
- Stretching
- Yoga

- Pilates
- Massage
- Rebounder

And …

Contrast Therapy – Taking the Plunge

Diary Note …

… steam rises in wisps, blurring the line between the snowy landscape and the pink dusk sky. I'm mid-soak in an outdoor onsen *after a vigorous ski day. The scent of mineral-rich spring water mingles with the earthy cedar stool and washing tub (a thorough scrub and cleanse part of the pre-soak bathing protocol). Water flows from deep in the earth through an age-darkened pipe – a soothing, rhythmic backdrop to the quiet stillness of the mountains.*

A Japanese traditional natural spring hot tub.

For a moment, the world is reduced to this perfect, serene balance – highlighting that profound experiences can be rooted in the simplest of elements. I then steel myself for the plunge into the adjoining ice bath.

Contrast therapy – the practice of alternating between heat and cold – isn't just a fad; it has stood the test of time across many cultures.

The ancient Romans had their caldarium and frigidarium, and for the Finns, the sauna is more than just a pastime; it's practically a national symbol. The art of temperature contrast runs in my veins. In the Netherlands, my father and his partner have sauna social evenings like we go to the pub. My mother's childhood holidays weren't complete without braving the icy waters of the North Sea – a tradition my eldest embraces with winter ocean swims. And my sister seeks out Alpine lakes so crisp and clear they redefine the word 'refreshing'.

Scientifically speaking – what's so great about switching between hot and cold? Research is compelling. Regular sauna use has been shown to lower blood pressure and reduce the risk of cardiovascular disease. Cold water immersion, on the other hand, is an immune booster. Studies suggest that those who regularly plunge into cold water have higher levels of antioxidant enzymes and fewer upper respiratory infections. The combination of hot and cold exposure sparks a vascular response, improving circulation and potentially reducing inflammation.

As for me? Now a firm advocate of the power of daily ice bath immersion. There's something undeniably invigorating about starting your day with a few minutes in water so brisk it momentarily steals your breath. On the days I skip, I feel the difference – my energy dips, and so does my clarity. Employing the Wim Hof breathing technique helps ease the initial shock, making the practice feel manageable.

Whether it's the icy grip of an ocean swim or the heat of a sauna, these moments remind me that vitality often hides on the other side of challenge.

The Wim Hof method combines deep breathing techniques with cold exposure, like ice baths, to boost energy, reduce stress, and improve overall wellbeing.

It feels incredible to step outside the cosseted ease we've built around ourselves.

TRY THIS

You don't need a Finnish sauna or a frigid mountain lake to get started.

- Start with 15 seconds of cold water at the end of your shower and work your way up.

- Consider investing in a small infrared sauna for home use. Pair it with a cool shower or a quick dip in a basin of iced water.

The key is to listen to your body. Start slow, give yourself time to adjust to the temperature swings, and trust the process – you might just find a new path to vitality.

Always check with your doctor before starting any new health practice, especially if you have underlying conditions.

Mid-Life Maintenance Mojo

Maintenance is what you have to do just so you can walk out the door knowing that if you go to the market and bump into a guy who once rejected you, you won't have to hide behind a stack of canned food.

– Nora Ephron

And isn't this the crux of it? Keeping up with the 'patch, patch, patch' after a certain point – another classic Nora line – can feel never-ending. But those small, daily acts make all the difference in how we feel – physically and emotionally.

My routine is extremely pared back – soap, water, a rich moisturiser which costs the price of a small car, sunscreen, a tinted base, mascara, and a great haircut. Yet when I am 'done' by my talented team for an event or photoshoot, the results through the camera lens are astounding. I barely recognise the well-put-together woman reflected back. So, I have relied on these expert friends for their tips, because as Bobbi Brown, make-up doyenne and wellbeing advocate, said, 'Maintaining simple self-care habits isn't just about appearances – it's about showing up for life with intention and confidence.'

Beauty on Your Own Terms

A deliberate act of self-respect. Whether you enjoy splurging on luxury products or prefer no-frills DIY methods, the goal is defining beauty on your terms and finding routines that fit *your* life, not society's expectations.

Take my mum, for example. She's mastered the art of no-frills beauty, ensuring more room in the budget for adventures. Her routine perfect in its simplicity: she trims her own hair, soaks her nails during the evening news, and exfoliates with a homemade scrub she swears by. Efficient and affordable.

She also starts every day with a post-shower, icy-cold splash.

So, whether your routine involves an expensive moisturiser or a home mani, it's the feeling it gives you that matters.

Now, let's hear from the experts...

The Joy of Getting Your Hair Right

Diary Note …

When I physically felt the best I had for decades, I made a visit to my hairdresser for a trim. Staring at myself in the mirror, a sense of urgency appeared. I'd been saving images of short sexy styles for years (not dissimilar to the best hair in my 'kid' photos. Note here:

when something works it works). God bless this gorgeous, successful young businesswoman, not wavering as I quivered 'Just cut it', adding for emphasis '... all of it' – she snipped until I was 30 cm lighter. Freeing. Cathartic. In the space of approximately two hours, I didn't recognise myself. I felt wild with purpose.

Having been forever 'defined' by my hair, I begin to brace for the potential changes as I age getting straight to the nub of things with Emily. 'Is it true that different products are more useful as our hair ages?' I ask.

'Yes and no. Hair certainly changes as we move through life – it's not just about colour shifting to silver. Hormonal changes can alter texture, thickness, and moisture levels too, making strands feel coarser. But it's deeply individual. What works for one person won't always suit another.'

Emily Brown, a colour and cutting professional with decades in the industry.

Weirdly, this swift change was THE thing that put the pep back in my step.

Breakout

Research tells us that hair ageing isn't just about aesthetics; changes in keratin production and scalp health can affect hair's ability to grow, retain moisture, and resist breakage. A well-rounded approach makes a difference – using products in moderation as well as nourishing hair from the inside with omega-3s, biotin, and antioxidants. Supplements like collagen or zinc may reduce thinning and improve strength.

Emily's Hair Wisdom: 5 Essential Tips

1. **Moisturise regularly.** Use leave-in conditioners or deep conditioning masks once a week to keep strands soft and prevent brittleness.

2. **Embrace your natural texture.** As hair changes, work with its natural wave or curl. Light layering adds movement and volume, especially if hair feels flat.

3. **Protect from heat damage.** Use a heat protectant spray, stick to low heat settings when styling. Air drying with a microfibre towel also reduces breakage.

4. **Maintain regular trims.** A well-cut style can make hair appear thicker and reduce split ends. Regular trims ensure hair stays healthy and manageable.

'Also, I recommend considering simple lifestyle adjustments like switching to satin or silk pillowcases,' Emily explains. 'These reduce friction while you sleep, helping to prevent frizz and breakage – especially for fragile strands. And don't neglect scalp health. A gentle scalp scrub can boost circulation and create a healthier environment for hair growth.'

Emily Brown is a renowned senior hairstylist, wowing Sydney's Eastern Suburbs with her award-winning salon Miss Brown (and namesake range of hair care), before moving to British Columbia, Canada, for love and a new legion of fans.

Expert: Dr Michele Squire – Begin with Your Skin

Let me point out – no matter what came before – there's something fabulous about healthy, radiant skin on an older woman.

Hormonal shifts can play havoc with our skin, so I asked Dr Michele Squire the big question: 'What can we do for our skin in mid-life if we are aiming for a dewy, juicy 'good health' glow?'

'As we age, our focus shouldn't be on erasing every wrinkle,' she begins. 'They're beacons of wisdom and experience – instead, it's about nurturing our skin's health and function.' During the course of our chat, I learn that whilst Michele's approach is scientific, she melds this with simplicity.

'Our skin undergoes changes from environment, lifestyle, genetics, and hormones. Over time, we see signs of ageing: collagen loss, pigmentation, broken capillaries, and fragile, dry skin that takes longer to heal. Luckily, there's a simple routine that holds the key to healthy skin as we age: sunscreen, cleanser, moisturiser, and vitamin A – and it doesn't need to cost a fortune.'

'Sunscreen is your #1 skincare product to prevent and treat ageing. Studies show that proper sunscreen use not only prevents damage but improves skin over time. Day-to-day UV exposure is responsible for 90% of visible skin ageing. Apply a teaspoon of SPF50+ sunscreen to your face, neck, ears, and chest every two hours, even indoors. You should go through a 50 ml sunscreen bottle every couple of weeks, so buy one that's affordable. Remember, sunscreen in make-up or moisturiser won't cut it.'

'Cleansers and moisturisers are a must, as hydration is key for

Middle sister battled spots as a teen, while my drier visage escaped scot-free. The last laugh? My skin now resembles papier-mâché, while sister – well, she's glowing.

Dr Michele Squire has a background in science and nursing. She founded Qr8, revolutionising the management of chronic skin conditions with evidence-based treatments and innovative technology.

healthy skin – as we age, skin gets drier. Moisturisers keep skin soft, smooth, and functioning well. Cleansers just need to clean your skin, so don't spend a fortune – an oil cleanser that rinses clean with warm water is best for removing sunscreen and make-up.'

Finally, vitamin A, or prescription retinoid, is as close to magic as skincare gets. 'It evens out skin tone and texture, stimulates collagen production, and helps plump out fine lines.' She pumps a little on to the back of her hand to show how easily it absorbs. 'Adding it to your routine replaces all the serums that promise results but don't deliver. And that's it,' she laughs. 'Simple and effective.'

She ends with sage advice that we might do well to follow before chasing 'youth in a bottle': 'Following the regimes I suggest provides clarity when faced with the overwhelming variety of skincare products promising eternal youth,' she says, before adding, 'most of which cannot deliver.'

Dr Michele Squire is a healthcare innovator with a background in science and nursing. She founded Qr8, revolutionising management of chronic skin conditions with evidence-based treatments and innovative technology. Dr Squire's commitment to patient outcomes makes her a pioneering force in skincare.

Make-up: The Art of 'Effortless' Effort

I maintain that, for special occasions and photographic shoots, it is best to book a professional to do the job – cue Sophia Ivy Lee.

She shares her tips for how we might spend the minimum time for maximum effect, even out a mid-life skin tone, add sparkle to tired eyes, a flush of good health to cheeks, and which products are worth spending money on.

With over 20 years' experience, Sophia is renowned for creating natural, flawless skin. She is the go-to make-up artist for photographers and directors.

Mid-life make-up tips from luxe to less:

1. **Natural light.** Buy a good high-magnification mirror (one on a small stand is fantastic for travel) and position yourself in natural light.

2. **Foundation.** Invest in a quality foundation. Less is more – a buffing brush or a dampened foundation sponge gives a more natural finish.

3. **Uneven skin tone.** Sparingly use concealer (ask an expert to match to your skin) to cover dark age spots or broken capillaries.

4. **Eyebrow shaping.** Professional eyebrow shaping can instantly lift the eyes and is the foundation of a fresher-looking visage.

5. **Avoid high-shimmer anything.** Specifically, eye make-up where it can settle in creases in an unflattering way.

An eyeshadow stick instead of powder lasts longer and is easy to blend with your finger or a brush.

6. **Lips.** A pop of colour on your lips is amazing for brightening your face. Take a look at women on Instagram of similar age, with similar hair colour and skin tone. Often, they have had a professional makeover, and you can see how different shades might be fun to try.

Sophia Ivy Lee, a Sydney-based freelance artist with 20-plus years of experience, is renowned for creating natural, flawless skin. She is the go-to make-up artist for photographers, directors, and private clients.

Tweakments

Lying in the middle ground between surgical intervention and an 'uber' facial is 'tweakments'. For years, I wondered what the resulting change in my visage would be should I ever be stranded on a desert island with prolonged 'all access barred' to my 'zhoosh' crew. When I turned fifty, I contemplated easing up – but never quite got around to cancelling the appointments. Then the universe read my mind and delivered COVID. I did eventually go back to my cosmetician – less often for less work, aiming for 'as Mother Nature intended', assuming she wants what is best for me. I focused on softening lines and plumping skin tone – the days of 'contouring' (weirdly high cheekbones and chubby cheeks for a woman in her fifties) a thing of the past.

Stick with what feels right, and above all, hand your precious face to verified professionals.

Just Wear the Bikini – Mid-Life Chic (How to Do Clothes)

Dressing with Intention

How we wear, what we wear, goes deeper than simply throwing on clothes and calling ourselves dressed.

The power of a good outfit cannot be underestimated. The right clothes can lift your mood and put a spring in your step. If you respect yourself enough to present your best version, there's a good chance the world will take notice. How others see us affects confidence, professionalism, relationships, and wellbeing.

In my opinion, society's standards in relation to dressing have relaxed to the point of comatose. A little less casual and anything goes, and a little more care would go a long way to repairing many of the world's woes (okay not the really, really important stuff… I mean the things like respect for self and others).

This is such an important topic it could reside further up the list of contents. How you dress speaks volumes about how you feel about yourself – studies show the impact of your choice of outfit on others' perception of you.

We all know people who command presence subtly, not loudly. I've rarely met anyone who doesn't want to present favourably. It's never too late, and it's not about looks or budget. You can't buy style – but you can learn it if it doesn't come naturally.

Research fashion icons like Trinny who are accessible, showcasing options from designer to high street.

Lyn Slater, author of *The Accidental Icon*, knows a thing or two about rewriting the rules of personal style. An academic who became a global fashion influencer in her sixties, Slater argues that personal style isn't just about following trends but about expressing who we are – and who we are becoming.

Her philosophy? If style evolves with us, mid-life fashion becomes a space for experimentation, not resignation. In her recent book, she explores the freedom that comes from rejecting outdated rules and embracing individuality. How much of your current wardrobe reflects who you truly are – or who you want to be?

Time to cast off the shackles of what you feel you 'should' be wearing and embrace what suits you best and makes you feel fabulous. Contrary to what you might think, I transformed my wardrobe before I started to look and feel better. It was a 'fake it 'til you make it' approach – except it wasn't fake. By mindfully choosing to put effort into my clothing, I noticed others took note.

Yes, activewear is comfortable, but did it have to become *everywhere* wear?

Have Fun with Fashion

Be bold, be brave, bring joy. What you wear can be a conversation starter. I've lost count of the fabulous encounters sparked by a stranger's compliment on my outfit. My wardrobe of kaftans has become a positive calling card. I also pay it forward; when I see someone with a great look, I take a moment to tell them how joyful their effort is to behold. At a time when society often expects us to fade into the background (after a certain age), I choose to stand up. When I felt invisible, paradoxically, I became more memorable …

A Grown Up's Gap Year Diary Note…

I'm in the Swiss Air lounge on a Monday morning, watching Europe and its entire luggage collection pass through. Finally, my flight is called, and after downing enough coffee to jumpstart the plane, I make a dash to the loo. Mid-kaftan hoisting, I hear a tentative 'Monique?' from the other side of the stall door.

'Um … yes?'

'I thought it was you – I saw which kaftan you had on today on Instagram.'

WTAF! An Instagram friend I'd been trying to meet in real life. She (and I) weren't meant to be in that spot that day – it was pure serendipity. If not for my distinctive travel-day attire, we might have passed each other like ships in the night (or travellers in an airport lounge). Instead, we had a delightful, unscheduled chat right there in the ladies' room ... that was fun!

Get 'Your Style', a Guide

Find your thing and take the guesswork out of getting dressed. Clear your wardrobe of clutter and get on with living, rather than wondering what to wear. The chicest women I know have a 'uniform' – they've figured out what works for them. This method can save hours each week.

Clothes need to be easy, comfortable, and chic. I've made peace with the styles and colours that suit me, and I refuse to suffer for fashion (I'm done with that). I care where my clothes come from, cull regularly, and no longer accumulate for the sake of it. In short, items need to fight hard for a spot in my wardrobe.

Less is more – lean towards classic, handmade pieces, with gaps filled by high street finds.

Breakout: Sustainable Fashion

A love and appreciation of fashion and textiles woven into my life story. My paternal grandparents arrived in New Zealand in the '50s as immigrants post-WWII, bringing to their new life their business of knitwear design and manufacture (down to weaving machinery and yarns). I grew up on the factory floor learning colour, pattern, and garment construction – quality versus 'fast fashion'. It was the arrival of the latter in the '70s that sealed the fate of the company – people wanted cheap and now, rather than classic and longevity.

Now, I'm not about to get all preachy on the topic – you decide what works for you (and of course I am not a puritan – I lean heavily toward purchasing classic and handmade, with wardrobe gaps made up of high street finds).

No-one gets it right all the time. Style is learned through practice, trial, and error. Take inspiration from style icons – Diana Vreeland was unconventional but personified style with her stack of bracelets, and Coco Chanel with her chic jersey suits. They may be from another era, but their timelessness can still be adapted today.

If you are not entirely certain you have 'nailed your style' ...

RIP Iris Apfel, whose late-in-life success proved that style transcends generations.

TRY THIS

Set aside half a day. Take everything out of the cupboards and onto the bed. If it's tatty – out. Too hard to style – out. Haven't worn it in 12 months – out. Wrong size – out. Keep only what makes you feel and look fabulous.

Take photos of various outfit combinations from your wardrobe – it's easier to assess through a lens than a mirror. Additionally, pay attention to what style and colours you're wearing when you receive compliments.

Learn to change the look of your outfits with accessories – fewer pieces, more combinations. Mend, clean, resole (shoes). Tatty is not how you're moving forward.

Plan seasonal edits. Store other season's garments elsewhere (or divide your wardrobe if space is tight) to make getting dressed quick and easy.

Consider Booking a Stylist

Like all 'experts', fashion stylists are not created equal. Do your homework and hire one whose style you admire not because it will necessarily work for you, but because if they have their own look together, they likely have the skills to sort yours. Many boutiques and department stores offer in-house stylists, often with fees that can be offset against any purchases.

It's a Fallacy That Looking Great Requires a Massive Budget

It requires a considered approach and some discipline: buy less, buy better. Pride of place in my wardrobe are artisanal dresses, Mum's beloved boots from 1975, a handcrafted Danish belt from my grandmother (circa 1935), and a few pairs of expensive shoes that get regular wear. It's better to have a few cherished pieces than a wardrobe full of 'never worn'. For the record, I've had times when I owned just one 'good dress and jacket' – so I'm not speaking from an ivory tower.

Circular fashion long part of my 'style kit bag' – my website has lists of fav designer seconds boutiques from around the globe

TRY THIS

1. Sign up to favourite designer sale notifications.

2. Sell unwanted garments (online or at local pre-loved and vintage stores).

3. Purchase from pre-loved fashion boutiques. Sustainable fashion now a welcome trend, one I've adopted for 30-plus years, first because I could not afford designer – and continued because I love circular fashion.

4. Hire outfits to wear and rent out your wardrobe too (thevolte.com).

My favourite find: a sweater my dad designed in 1975 I found for sale on eBay in the US – still pristine. That made my heart sing.

Buy 'Out of Season' Fashion's ever-turning wheel demands cash flow, hence the constant sales. I'm happy to shop past seasons and reap the savings. Who needs to be a slave to trends?

Best Foot Forward A good pair of shoes can take your look from fine to fabulous. Most of my clothing budget goes on footwear – with no tolerance for discomfort! Heels are rare; stylish flats and dressy sneakers are now my mainstays. Walking miles in style? Yes, please.

Shop Local Local boutiques carefully curate their stock, meaning you won't spot everyone in your neighbourhood wearing the same thing. Shop small, look chic.

High Street with Cred I'm a fan of Uniqlo for basics – good quality, simple aesthetic, and a solid ethos. Find similar high street brands that align with your values and style.

The Potency of a Professional Photoshoot

This is about feeling 'en pointe'. Note I said 'feeling' – not looking.

Diary Note…

One of the best decisions I made stepping back into professional life was overhauling 'my brand', although, at the time, I didn't realise that's what I was doing. Building layer upon layer the 'version' of me that showed up as the refreshed woman I was beginning to embody. During this time, I spied a portrait of a woman in a national newspaper. The natural, beautifully shot image struck me, and I tracked down the talented photographer (Sally Flegg). It took four months to secure a photoshoot, giving me plenty of time to nearly talk myself out of it.

I thought of every reason why I didn't want to stand in front of a camera. But I talked myself off the ledge by treating myself as a

PROJECT (remember, we've had this conversation). As I had done many moons ago for clients. No experience in life is ever wasted.

So, do 'it' anyway, and don't overthink it. My self-doubt nemesis still chats away, but as Elizabeth Gilbert expresses in Big Magic: *'Put her in the backseat – thank her for her input – then politely ask her to shhhhhhhh.'*

There's nothing like standing in swimmers under bright lights to help locate a new fierceness and decide not to waste another minute under a cloak of 'I can't'.

When you step away into a smaller world, it can be easy to forget what came before. Your capabilities. Now not all of us 'want back in' – but if you do – gift yourself a personal brand update and project your best self. It does look great AND feels even better. Whether you use the images for professional or personal purposes matters not.

TRY THIS

Sally Flegg Photo Shoot Tips

1. Prepare three different looks – from casual to smart – to give you versatility during the shoot.

2. Mix textures, block colours, and a few neutrals. Fitted clothes generally work better, as baggy ones don't always translate well on camera.

3. If possible, hire a stylist for a few hours (or have an online session) to help you nail down the perfect outfits.

4. If your budget allows, book a hair and make-up artist for a natural look. It not only takes the pressure off, but it also gives you a chance to pick up some great tips.

5. Don't rely solely on recommendations – research photographers whose style aligns with the images you want.

6. During the shoot, trust your photographer to guide you. They know how to capture your best angles, so relax and enjoy the experience.

Sally Flegg is a Sydney-based photographer specialising in natural light headshots. With over 20 years of experience, she has worked with top agents and acting graduates both in Australia and the USA.

SPRING POSSIBILITIES

As you conclude the Spring – *Feel Reinvigorated* section, reflect on your new-found energy. The chapters guided you through key steps toward renewal:

1. **Feeling Better** Establishing regimes aligned with your values and goals to set the stage for a reinvigorated life.

   ### TRY THIS

   Set aside five minutes today to tune in to how your body feels. Are you hungry, tired, or tense? Make one small change – whether it's eating something nourishing, taking a nap, going for a nature walk, or stretching sore muscles.

2. **Nutrition Basics for Your Body** Fuel in a way that supports both immediate and long-term health.

   ### TRY THIS

   At your next meal, try to stop eating when you feel about 80% full. Practise this mindful eating method once a day this week and observe how it affects your digestion and satisfaction.

3. **Movement and Strength** Understand how 'getting strong' and 'movement' contribute to overall wellbeing and make them a daily practice.

TRY THIS

Choose a form of movement you enjoy (walking, dancing, strength training, yoga, or a home workout). Block 20 minutes in your calendar for this activity every day for the next week. Set a phone reminder and keep a daily note – how do you feel after each session?

4. **Rest and Mental Health** Establish a strong foundation for sleep and mindfulness and embrace the Dutch practice of *niksen* (doing nothing).

TRY THIS

Make one change to your bedroom to support better sleep – blackout curtains, using a fan for white noise, separate beds, or investing in a comfortable pillow.

5. **Mojo and Chic** A mid-life makeover; rediscover your personal style and find joy in redefining your presence in the world.

TRY THIS

Create a mood board of style inspirations. Then, head to the shops and try on a variety of outfits. Photograph yourself and spend time reflecting on what suits you and how your current wardrobe works (or needs refreshing).

SUMMER
FEEL ADVENTUROUS

Time to feel freer – explore adventure – recharge, build confidence, experiment, travel – a season of energy.

Practically speaking, Summer is the season to:

1. Learn to rediscover your courage. Be brave.

2. Ignite excitement for your future through new experiences.

3. Take some time out for YOU – start small, dream big.

4. Explore solo travel as a path to self-discovery.

5. Research different options that fit your interests and budget.

For a person who, 'pre-kids', had a work life 'on a plane every week', it seems astonishing I segued so easily into a grounded life. An odd sensation to be 'back on the road', travelling, not simply holidaying in a spot – the world shiny and curious again.

I become as I was 25 years ago – before husband, before children. Back when I was more spontaneous, more daring, more fun, more unwavering. By day, cliff-top parachuting, by night, dancing – twilight illuminating the swaying crowd. I sleep naked with curtains open, wanting to wake early to the sunrise so as to not miss a minute.

Monique xx

A Grown Up's Gap Year Cautionary Tale

A Grown Up's Gap Year Diary Note … *On the eve of running (even further) away …*

… solo time in the Whitsundays turned into a loving upheaval when my darlings arrived for a hot meal and a hug, because the fridge was full, the weather warm, and they missed me. Except, I still missed me, too, and really didn't want to be derailed before I even began the search. So, six months after those lightbulbs were changed, it became time to hit the road again. Further away …

Hastily booked within two weeks, the trip to Europe left just enough time to choose new sunnies, and not enough to begin second-guessing. That is, until the eve of departure – when the scales tipped in favour of trepidation, outweighing adventure or excitement. I took to voicing my nerves on Instagram and was flooded with messages of positivity: *I was nervous too but learned to relax into the unknown and relish new-found joy. Once you're there, you'll be fine!* They were right! But first, there was the ever-circling question – what kind of mother just scoots into the sunset?

When I began writing this book, I googled 'why mid-life women run away' and found a name for it – 'depleted mothers/carers syndrome'. No shit, Sherlock! I would say that sums up the majority of women with a full calendar of commitments. Digging a little deeper, it seems the main way men 'get away' is a planned sabbatical. Listen, take it from me, when you are exhausted from giving, the last thing you want to do is 'plan your departure', requiring pre-trip scheduling on the home front only to return picking up the pieces – what actually seems the point? Now, I'm certain these lovely researcher types mean well – but have they considered the possibility that a little spur-of-the-moment away time is simply the response to 'cannot do another bloody thing for another person syndrome'?

Risky? Yes, but ...

Not everyone will come on board with your 'hunt for space'. Be prepared for others not to understand; your change is their change. Patience may be needed while they catch up – or not.

Despite the risks, I couldn't *not* go. The longing for freedom wouldn't abate. I weighed the fear of disrupting my marriage or being misunderstood, or judged against feeling lost if I did nothing. What a waste of life.

From Small Things ... YOU Might Grow

You're toying with taking time out, but overwhelmed? Break it down. Are you afraid of others' reactions? Guilt? Uncertainty? Acknowledge those fears, but don't let them rule. Sometimes the biggest risk is not taking one at all. The space you create for yourself could breathe new life into your relationships, your sense of purpose, your happiness. Life is filled with obligations, but it's possible to shift and make space for yourself first, so you show up feeling gracious, less resentful, and more enthusiastic. This shift isn't easy after decades of habits – a work in progress.

How To Share Your Need for Space

On a ski lift recently, I chatted to a couple of gentlemen on a 'mates' holiday.

It was a long, slow lift with time for conversation.

'What do you do?' one asked me.

'I've written a guidebook for women, to take action when they feel they've gone missing – from their lives,' I said.

'So then, can you help me answer a question?' asked the chap. 'What do I need to do to help my wife be happier? That's all I want for her, for us.'

A decent elevator pitch has never been my strong suit – but you get the drift.

It's not the first time I have been asked this question. When I returned from my extended, ahem, disappearance from the family, messages began; colleagues of my husband who had noted my reinvigoration – they were feeling lost amidst the changes the women in their lives were exploring, the rug had been pulled out from under them and they had no idea how to navigate this new normal for them or their partners. Given time constraints, 'Give them space' was the best I could offer to my new friends on the lift. I did want to query as to the part they felt they played in their partner's 'mid-life malaise' and, indeed, how they too might feel about their own choices – but we would have needed many more minutes to tackle this.

At the risk of generalising, I observe women finally free of 'caring' go wild with possibility while their (male) partners want to retreat to a solid group of 'mates' and predictable pursuits. They may genuinely struggle to keep up with us, puzzled at our vim and vigour, and yes, wondering whether this newly minted formidable, confident partner is here to stay.

Although we never stop caring, so perhaps it might be better stated as a moment away from the mental load.

I say yes!

As I travelled for my extended 'moment', I made many new friends, constantly subdued by their incredulity – different languages, same question: 'What were the words I used to explain to my husband that I needed a breather?'

'Relationships can mean many things,' I told them. 'A need for space included.'

Breakout

Think about all the mums, sisters, friends in your life – when we put our mind to it, we are incredibly capable of creating the changes we want to affect. There is much maligned in 'maledom' – however, amidst this are very, very good men, too.

I love the men in my life and hopefully, you have some great guys in yours, too.

It should not be 'us versus them', so there is work ahead. I wonder how we can collectively help shape a positive future narrative.

And Then ...

But what if you can't just pack up and leave? What if your life has you anchored firmly in place? Exploring isn't about miles travelled. The most profound journeys happen right where we are.

I recently had a conversation with a friend who was feeling stagnant and looking for advice on finding adventure without upending family life. 'You've just started swimming again,' I reminded her. 'Why not try every pool nearby, a new one every week?' This being Sydney, Australia, we swiftly gathered around 20 'doable' locations – ocean pools, indoor pools, the sea. She loved this and I am happy to report she is still swimming and loving the adventure of bringing novelty to her everyday.

We'll explore 'micro-novelties' in more depth – ideas to shake up daily routines and perspectives, proving that you don't have to leave your city – or even your suburb – for life to feel fresh again.

Coupled and Living Apart

For the most part, I don't live with my husband. We co-habit (with the kidults) in intervals, and then I soar intermittently for some space. I've made myself dizzy from 'needs must' back and forth. But, so be it; a small price to pay as it works for us, for now.

On any given day, I field questions – mostly incredulous or curious – about living apart from my spouse. They run the gamut:

- **Incredulity:** '*How the hell do I get some space for myself?*' Keep reading the book.

- **Doubt:** '*So, you're still married but don't live together full-time?*' Correct. (Side note: this isn't exactly a new idea. Decades ago, my Oma, widowed in her seventies, agreed to move in with her long-term boyfriend – with one caveat: separate townhouses next door to each other. After raising five children and living with a handful of a husband, she, too, craved space.)

- **Acceptance:** '*Cool idea if everyone's happy.*'

- This arrangement—coined *living apart together* (LAT)—is more common than I realised when I first 'fled.' I had no frame of reference then; no one in my circle was doing the same. However research now shows that LAT arrangements can strengthen long-term relationships.

The thread that binds The Husband and me is strong, also elastic enough to allow us to drift freely separately for now.

Let's be clear: this is not about seeking new partners or a divorce without the paperwork.

The Husband has his interests and mates, and I have mine. We travel separately for the most part.

Together, we share two gorgeous young men, a puppy, holidays, and decades of heartache and happiness.

It's about giving each other the freedom to pursue individual passions while still choosing to sail through life together. Mid-life sharpens the horizon – ensure you're both steering toward joy.

TRY THIS

Yes, this is your moment; however, if you are in a relationship, it is important for your partner to be on board. My advice is 'do as I say, not as I did' – I announced I was off after I had left. Whilst it is not the time for 'asking permission' once you are clear about what it is you want to do – what 'space' looks like for you – a mature and infinitely more successful approach is to take time to write a letter to your partner explaining how you feel, what you hope they will come on board with, and what your plans are. Only you will know what is appropriate for your situation. This may also be a time you require professional relationship assistance.

Mid-life coupling is put under the microscope in Autumn, with tips from relationship expert Lissy Abrahams.

The Not-So-Frivolous Folly of Running Away

A Grown Up's Gap Year Diary Note...

My actual fleeing no more planned, or longed for, than a swift realisation lineated is how I live, and frankly, probably expect to drop off my perch. I've lost the ability to be creative with myself.

Research shows that the search for the 'thing' missing in mid-life is predominantly the driver in the getaway car. In my case, my airport chauffeur my twenty-year-old son, who, after a quick hug for his wild-eyed mum, gave a toot, a wave, and a slightly concerned look in the rearview mirror before heading home to his dad, younger brother, and our dog.

This urge to 'escape' in mid-life may look like a cliche, yet it isn't just anecdotal – it's backed by science – life satisfaction follows a U-shaped curve, consistently dipping in our forties and fifties before rising again, and often manifesting as a desire for radical change.

Could It Be Hereditary?

I grew up with stories of mid-life bolting kinfolk, and yet it never occurred to me to 'follow in their footsteps'. Parallels only came to me later when teasing apart ideas for the book, memories bubbling to the surface – the 'aha' revealed via a recurring theme: the hereditary propensity for disappearance.

A great-grandfather vanished for decades, leaving behind a wife and children, only to return when ill health came knocking (there isn't space to finish this tale …). My paternal Oma, an only child of doting parents, sought the farthest point from her roots in Holland. She sailed to New Zealand, her ship piled high with a designer kit house, a car, family heirlooms, a husband, and four children under eight. She may have left, but she took 'home' with her – parts of ourselves we can never truly escape.

But it is my Papa's story that captures familial wanderlust. At seventy-five, an age when most are settling into the comfort of routine, he packed his essentials, distributed 'inheritance' items among my sisters and me, and returned to his country of birth.

Stubbornness and not much else I can glean as her motivator.

237

The pull was irresistible, a siren call that echoed across decades and continents. During one long phone chat, I asked him what compelled him to leave behind his daughters, grandchildren, and the life he'd built.

'It wasn't a whim or a crisis,' he began. 'It was a homecoming in the deepest sense – a decision not taken lightly because I knew in gaining a place where everything felt familiar, I also risked losing, but ...' His voice trailed off.

I completed the sentence for him. '... you couldn't not go?'

'Yes, exactly,' he replied. '... and there is Heleen!' His teenage 'gap year' girlfriend whom he returned for, reunited in their seventies.

I remember the mix of emotions as we said goodbye – sadness at the distance that would separate us, and a strange sense of understanding – a reflection of that same restlessness that suddenly came upon me. It wasn't about escaping his life here; it was about reclaiming a part of himself he'd set aside. In leaving, he taught us that it's never too late to answer the call of your true self.

Not Seeking Greener Pastures

Yet my own journey diverged from these family tales in one crucial aspect. My 'running away' was always meant to be temporary. In pursuit of a breather, a chance to reinvigorate a sense of fun and adventure. Wisdom shows that life-changing moments aren't always mapped out. So, I set off with no real plan, allowing myself to spend each 24 hours as I saw fit. My life, my choices – not seeking greener pastures, just a fresh perspective – freedom preferable without an objective. I do encourage you to 'get away'. It's not frivolous, it's definitely freeing, and it is not a folly.

The 'Pray' Bit of My Runaway

I was raised in a household of two different religions, an undercurrent of familial tension – one side of the family deeply pious. By the time I was eight, I'd concluded that perhaps it was all a bit of a crock and proudly declared myself an atheist. Yet even then, I found myself drawn to the edges of spiritual exploration – spending Saturday mornings as a tween, watching the Hare Krishnas dance through the streets of our Fiji home, mesmerised by their robes (kaftan love even then), the incense (a pattern here), and their sense of purpose (aha!).

I'm not suggesting this remains my belief today – that's a deeply personal matter – but to highlight how different seasons of life bring different perspectives.

Later, when we were dating, I announced (to now hubby) I was undertaking a four-year 'conversion' to his religion. He begged me not to, the memory still fresh on an orthodox childhood to which he had no desire to return. But I 'felt called', a desire to connect future children to a cultural and spiritual lineage. (Sidebar: Much later, my maternal grandmother declared a long-held secret on her deathbed that her family was originally of this faith – further credence to 'when you get a gut feeling …').

Never about religion per se – more an exploration of 'otherness'.

Here is where I should state another branch of this theme: my history with soothsayers. Essentially, all roads lead back to seeking clarity whilst feeling lost – with a fixation on seeking out fortune tellers. From the gloomy predictions of the elderly philosopher that read my palm at the Taj Lake Palace in Udaipur to Victoria, the sage who sent me packing home from London. In a tiny alley in the middle of Tokyo, I fed questions to a clairvoyant via Google Translate (questions and answers predictably all lost in translation). In Singapore, 'visions' from a woman who had clearly spent the morning on Instagram (verbatim from my ten latest posts). In Hong Kong, travelling with my husband, I visited a guru. Good fortune-telling etiquette dictates that you do not sit in on someone's reading. An exception was made on that occasion in the interests of marital 'full disclosure'. As we settled in, I suggested (hissed) to the Husband not to breathe scepticism over the experience. Unable to help himself, he interrupted the flow midway to ask for clarification. I sensed increasing frustration from my soothsayer as the Husband probed further, 'Does my wife's fortune show an actual windfall?' What he meant was, did it seem likely my constant investment in seeking the fortunes of my future would render results, allowing him to spend the remainder of his days on a golf course.

'No,' was the guru's terse response. 'Your wife shows much creative energy, not money.'

It seemed all the distraction mixed up my aura. Speechless, I swiftly moved on to the incense-scented temple.

I 'gravitated' to many a sage encounter because I was stuck – it felt less problematic to pay (beg) someone to make a decision for me. If things in my life then went array, or I elected for the status quo – 'misguidance' could be blamed. When you feel lost, or cannot seem to make up your mind, it doesn't do harm to look for answers

– although I may have finally concluded all transcendence leads to the same spot. You are precisely where you should be, for that time. You simply may feel comfort in seeking clarity from another while musing on your options, whether from spirituality or soothsayers. I like the Dalai Lama 's view 'My religion [spirituality] is very simple. My religion is kindness.'

Remember our conversation on signing up for 'shiny' courses when searching for guidance.

Breakout

One morning during my Whitsundays 'escape', I stepped outside to find a tawny owl and her baby nestled in the palm tree at my front door. In the two decades of owning the house I had never seen an owl, and I haven't spotted one since. This unexpected encounter felt deeply symbolic, as owls often emerge during challenging times to serve as guides – conveying truth, understanding, patience, and wisdom, especially when life feels tumultuous. Another reminder that clarity and guidance can come from anywhere during periods of upheaval and distress.

Another 'sign'. When going over old journal entries for this book a daily mantra card I'd been gifted during my travels fluttered out, *The Sun*. I do not recall where or when it came into my possession. When I investigated its meaning, I learned it is the symbol for positivity and optimism – I love this!

Call them what you will – spiritual signposting works for me.

Going It Alone

Leaving on a Jet Plane

A Grown Up's Gap Year Diary Note ...

At check-in, I watch a young man drop his backpack on the scales.

'Off for a gap year,' he tells the airline rep.

Me too, *I add silently. I quell the urge to call the eldest – get him to turn the car around, a dreadful mistake made. His mum a silly, hormonal twit, and a sceptic, I profess to have been vaguely distrusting of people 'off to find themselves', scoffing at the flakiness of it.*

I'm travelling, not running – I say ad nauseum. Others see it differently. But to be fair? Same, same – leaving A to discover something new at B.

Yet here I am, uncertainty, overwhelm, exhaustion, and a side order of guilt threatening to derail the expedition before I make it through customs. Once 'on the other side,' the weight starts to lift. An hour later, buoyed by a sense of hope blended with a shot of airport caffeine, I join the throng moving toward the departure gate. I'm on my way.

Travel offers space to think, the distance to reflect, and a chance to step outside the confines of familiarity. If you are craving quiet contemplation, truly committed to 'getting away', go lightly, my friend.

This includes your choice of companions. If you want to be amongst besties and loved ones, book a family holiday, a girl's getaway, a romantic partner's trip, a dinner out – whatever it is that works for everyone. Note the last few words, 'works for everyone'.

The best friendships and loves are about anticipating one another's needs, knowing intuitively without having to speak the words – a basis for the strongest relationships. You are an incredible friend; I know you are. Nothing replaces the comfort and deep love for old friends.

Yet new acquaintances who know nothing of our background, or baggage, are worth cultivating. A fresh meeting of minds is invigorating, humbling, and perhaps 'just what you need'.

'A Grown Up's Gap Year' style of travelling differs from a mere 'holiday'. If you are taking time to reinvigorate yourself, let you be the centre of your days. The gift I recommend you give yourself is to please no-one but you. You do not want other people's timetables, preferences, problems, cheerleading, comfort levels – take their love and blessings. Just leave them at home. You will have so much more to offer when you return.

Learning What You Love to Do Again

Two of the most valuable souvenirs I brought home were first, remembering how to get comfortable with being uncomfortable. When you are 'coupled', there is a propensity to get lazy – not much effort is required when you have a companion on tap. Honing an ability to sit with myself, alongside new acquaintances, without performance (the Husband calls it my 'performing seal routine').

A sense that my worth to others is linked to an ability to 'entertain and fill the spaces'.

Or rather, this is when we could be putting in the effort, but rarely do – to keep things fresh. More on this later.

I'm often asked, 'what did you do with your days?' The truth is it wasn't the *doing* that mattered as much as the *being*.

And the second? Remembering what I love to do.

One mid-summer Croatian morning, I am reminded of this by Dragar (a portly gentleman with a strong Baltic accent) – watching my hesitation at the sea wall two days running. 'Eighty years I swim here. Jump!' he calls. Mid-leap, I release the grip on my antipodean radar – deep water, sea creatures – plunging deep in the crystal Adriatic. Silvery bubbles as I break the surface, I inhale sharply, tasting salt and adrenaline. I love to leap – when had I forgotten this?

New People

Diary Note …

I've missed the stimulation of other places, new people.

Meeting kindred spirits around the globe, connections can be as shallow or deep as you decide without any pressure to invest emotionally. Some fleeting, brief exchanges; the great 'bear' of a Venetian who served up my simple home-cooked fare for several evenings; St Marco glowing gold in the fading daylight as we chatted about his escape from the small neighbourhood as a young man (you couldn't have kicked me out of his quaint corner of Venice, but there you have it … one person's brown, another's green). His fascination at my departure later in life, and my fascination with his mum, who he had returned from travel to care for. Sharing a love of wanderlust and sun setting over water. Will he remember our conversation? Probably not, but that is not the point. I do, and every exchange like this expanded me, took me closer to better understanding the vast beauty of this world.

And learn her recipes – I have one for you.

Travelling alone, you strike up conversation with more abandon:

- Flavia leaves her husband to go to her home overseas many months a year. She has a younger friend – in fact, she has had a string of 'friends'. 'No-one right for me,' she admits. 'Actually, maybe I want no-one.' Her 175-year-old renovated farming house is all she needs right now.

- Jakov, my boat driver – handsome in a slightly scruffy way. I watch as he swims in the Adriatic, declining the offer to join him. I entertain for a brief moment a liaison – but no – complication is not part of this itinerary. Instead, I appreciate his lean brown muscles and listen to him chat about his young family – leaving him an uncomplicated large tip.

- And then there was Suki, the waitress at my hotel. We spoke often of our sons. On my last day, she hugged me, sobbing quietly about her absent boy. At that moment, our stories diverged: I was heading home to mine; she was not. Fleeting encounters like this one can linger far longer than we expect, reminding us of our own good fortune.

New Places

There are few experiences that trump a first morning in a new destination. Waking early for a long 'getting to know the neighbourhood' walk, coffee at a local spot, and getting the lay of the land before most arise. Do this for a few days in a row and you'll find yourself nodding in recognition to fellow early birds or a barista who recalls your order. I tend to look for walking tours (cooking, art, hiking, cultural), a magnet for other solo travellers and a lovely way to feel connected.

Travelling alone, my senses are heightened. I listen – to the wind, the sea, the distant murmur of evening conversation. I observe, taste, and appreciate every nuance of my surroundings.

A Guide for Solo Travel

Solo travel teaches you to follow your instincts, make spontaneous decisions, and find joy in the unexpected. Yes, there are challenges: being stuck at the table near the loo or paying the dreaded 'singles tax'. But it allows the freedom to advocate for yourself, ask for what you need, and be unapologetically in charge of your own experience.

Travel Agent. I cannot emphasise how valuable this relationship is for ensuring smooth travel arrangements. Any trip more complicated than point-to-point flights, my travel guru is on speed dial (and worth any consulting fee she requires to deliver the service).

Research. Do your homework. Spend time reading suggestions from seasoned solo female travellers. Websites are packed with valuable insights and real-world advice.

Ease in. Not ready to fly solo? Consider a small group tour. My mum did this in Morocco in her sixties and loved the ease of this style of adventure.

Check out women-led trips in Australia – Jean @GlamGirls LuxTravels, and Melinda @ Pineapple Villa.

Connect locally. 'Meet with locals' groups. A coffee and a good chat can turn into your most authentic experience.

Safety first. Trust your instincts and stay aware of your surroundings. Research local customs, dress codes, and opt for safe transport options.

Journal the journey. Start a travel journal or blog – you'll love reading later what it reveals about your transition.

Learn a few phrases. Learn language basics. A few key phrases in the local language will go a long way in making new friends.

Book social accommodation. Stay where people mingle. Choose accommodation with communal spaces or organised activities. You might find yourself swapping stories with fellow solo travellers over dinner.

Self-date. Plan something special for you in every new destination. Maybe it's that pottery class, or a dreamy lunch you've always wanted to try.

Capture your solo adventure with a local professional photoshoot – let them document your glow-up.

Eat with locals. Join apps like Eatwith for authentic local dining experiences. It's the perfect way to enjoy regional cuisine and meet some fascinating new people. I love local 'in-home' cooking classes and have written lots of articles about these experiences and the new friends I've made this way.

Daily interaction. Challenge yourself to have at least one brief exchange with someone new every day – whether it's a shopkeeper or someone in a café. You never know where a small conversation might lead.

Pack light but smart. A pair of killer shades and a silk scarf – they can elevate any look, even if you've been living out of a suitcase for weeks.

Someone who basks in idle time and observes their surroundings.

Mindful travel. Slow it down, wander aimlessly through local neighbourhoods, sip a coffee at a café, and just *be a flâneuse.*

You Can Do Extraordinary Things Anywhere

The human desire to seek the extraordinary isn't just wanderlust – it's wired into our DNA. Dr Dacher Keltner's research into 'awe' reveals that experiencing wonder, whether in far-flung places or our own backyards, fundamentally changes how we see ourselves and our world.

Found in his book *The New Science of Everyday Wonder and How It Can Transform Your Life.*

Many of us long for a taste of 'elsewhere' – even just for a moment. A chance to try on a different life mantle and see how it fits. We are drawn to books like *Eat, Pray, Love* and *Wild* or films like *Under the Tuscan Sun;* there's something alluring about venturing into the unknown.

Nuance of Novelty

It matters not where or how far you travel – the farther commonly the worse – but how much alive you are.

– Henry David Thoreau

Let's not make any of this too hard. You don't have to leave your city – or even your suburb – for life to feel fresh again. As simple as trying a new hobby (I found the thrill of ocean kayaking two suburbs away – that I barely paddled past the bay's edge mattered not). The possibilities are endless. I like to call them micro-novelties.

After all, the best stories often begin with the words 'I decided to try something different …'.

It's not the destination but the change in routine that makes us feel alive – also termed 'microjoys' by author and positive thinking expert Cyndie Spiegel.

TRY THIS

1. **Morning music ritual.** Research shows that music boosts everything from sleep quality to mood. Explore your neighbourhood with a new playlist in your ears.

2. **The anonymous café.** Find a coffee shop several suburbs away where you can be gloriously anonymous. Bring a book or journal, or simply sit and people-watch.

3. **Random bus adventure.** Go to your local bus stop (or train or ferry) and board the first that arrives, regardless of its destination. Ride it to the end of the line, then explore that area; discover hidden gems in your own city.

4. **Creative pursuit.** Sign up for a one-day workshop in something you've always wanted to try – pottery, painting, writing. It's a break from routine and a chance to explore a new side of yourself.

5. **Awe walk.** Take your usual route but notice what makes you pause – morning light painting shadows, architecture you've missed in passing, a resilient plant breaking through concrete – approaching the familiar with wonder can be as powerful as exploring new territory.

6. **Local tourist.** Spend a day exploring your own city as if you were a tourist. Visit that museum you've been meaning to check out or try a restaurant in a neighbourhood you rarely visit.

7. **Dawn patrol.** Wake up before sunrise and find a local vantage point to watch the day begin. Bring a thermos of coffee or tea and journal your thoughts as the world awakens around you.

Scientists have found even brief moments of awe – whether trying something new or seeing the familiar with fresh eyes – can reduce stress and increase our sense of connection.

These small steps often lead to greater leaps. I find myself drawn to mid-life women doing extraordinarily interesting things in fascinating places. They might claim they're 'no-one special', but to me, they're trailblazers – following paths I might never have considered. The following women did just that – embracing lifestyle changes, solo travel, or entirely new careers. Let their stories inspire your journey, one small adventure at a time.

Women Doing Interesting Things in Fascinating Places

In my mid-twenties, while working a serious five-star hotel job, I encountered a corporate client who defied the usual drab business garb with bright, bold clothes that radiated purpose. Her name was Geraldine Cox AM, and although I had no idea of her story at the time, I sensed it must be a good one. Much later, I learned she was the remarkable founder of Sunrise Cambodia, an orphanage and family support organisation in Cambodia. She had lived in Phnom Penh in the 70s, and that profound experience had left its mark.

The older, wiser me wants to ask her about her courageous decision. What drove her in her fifties to leave behind the conventional and dive into something so challenging and rewarding as setting up an orphanage in a foreign land? Throughout my career, I've met many successful people, but it's the later-in-life adventurers who truly captivate me. These women remind us that life doesn't end at 50, 60, 70, or beyond – it simply takes on new hues. They fascinate me because they embody courage, resilience, and the joy of reinvention. Their stories show us the transformative power of embracing change and following our hearts, no matter our age or circumstances.

Life, Your Way

Michelle Cox is testament to living authentically and staying open to change. Balancing life as an executive director in tourism with creative passions like pottery and writing, her philosophy is clear: life isn't about following someone else's version of success – it's about designing a life that fits you.

Following my interview on her podcast – I turn the mic around, asking what motivated her leap from corporate to creative?

'I've always been creatively inclined, but hadn't found *my thing*,' she pauses. 'When I turned 50 – three years older than my mum was when she died – it hit me. I couldn't keep waiting to explore what sparked joy, so I jumped in. I took piano lessons, learned to read music, and signed up for local workshops. One of those was a pottery course I finished just before the COVID lockdown. I had a bag of clay in the boot of my car, time on my hands, and YouTube tutorials at my fingertips. That's how it began – organically.'

What started as a playful experiment soon grew into something more. 'I didn't set out to build a business,' she laughs. 'I just wanted to make my own dinner set! But taking a 'try-and-see' approach led me somewhere unexpected. I tell other women to do the same – don't wait, just try. You'll never know what lights you up until you explore. Living authentically is liberating – and youthful. It's about doing things differently at this stage and playing with possibilities. Yes, it can feel scary to change course, but if it feels right, just take the plunge.'

As we continue chatting, we land on a shared passion – travel. 'Travel has been my University of Life,' Michelle says. 'It's where I've learned the most – about people, resilience, and myself. I've heard all the excuses from people, why they 'can't travel right now'. My response remains firm. I've watched friends overcome challenges to make it happen – saving for years, renting out their homes, even taking their children out of school to live abroad. Where there's a will, there's a way.'

Beyond her personal explorations, Michelle also mentors younger people: 'I had great role models who paved the way for me, and now I love paying it forward. Giving your time to others is a gift, and it's something we can embrace in mid-life. The freedom to live differently, to take risks and follow passions – that's where the real fun begins.'

Michelle Cox is a corporate leader, author, and creative entrepreneur who challenges societal norms. Her podcast is called 'One Question'. Michelle's philosophy is to live authentically and embrace lifelong learning.

Each episode revolves around one question: 'If there was one thing you think society should talk more about, what would it be?'

Her term for mid-life? 'Middle youth'. I'm adopting this!

Embracing Middle Youth

Artist Desiree Prinsloo embodies redefining life on her terms. We talk on the phone as she sits in her restored house on Hydra – a place she now calls home for summers. Life, as she puts it, had given her a hard shove off course – and it was in the aftermath that she decided to start over on a small Greek island.

'After my husband passed, the unravelling was ... well, monumental, I had nothing left to lose by the end of it, so one night, scrolling through property listings in Greece and Italy, I thought, *Why not?* And that was it. Within a week, I packed my things and left.'

She said it so decisively, with a sense of inevitability, that it strikes me that this kind of leap isn't always born from whimsy. Sometimes, it's survival.

Hydra wasn't a random choice; she'd been coming to the island for years. But buying her own home – one in dire need of repair – was something else entirely. 'I stayed on through a freezing winter to restore it,' she says, describing endless days of work with two local tradesmen, neither of whom spoke much English. 'Somehow, we understood each other perfectly. We kept everything simple – raw wood, whitewashed walls. To let the light in and leave space for life to unfold.'

'It's freeing,' she adds. 'No-one here cares who you are or what you left behind. Everyone's got a story – mine's just one of many.' With a 40-year award-winning art career, Desiree has founded art societies, tutored artists, and written for art magazines – her work exhibited globally. Now, Desiree runs intimate artist and writers retreats from her studio. 'I love watching others transform, find clarity, or simply reconnect with their creativity – it reminds me that reinvention can happen at any stage in life. Look at me; I moved here in my sixties.'

She goes on to tell me about evenings spent painting, windows thrown open to the salty breeze, the same light that once drew

Leonard Cohen to this place spilling into her studio. 'Look,' she continues, 'people think moving to an island is some kind of romantic fantasy – but there are challenges. It's not always easy, but it feels right. And that's enough.' When I ask what advice she'd give to anyone longing for a similar change, she doesn't hesitate: 'Don't wait for the perfect moment. It won't come. You'll never have every answer.' As a parting thought, Desiree adds, 'I tell everyone to swim, every day, in the ocean – that's where the real restoration happens.'

Dream Versus Reality: Owning a Home Abroad

Desiree offers practical advice and candid insights. 'It sounds romantic, and it is, but you need to approach it with open eyes,' she cautions.

Her tips are straightforward and invaluable:

- **Hire a trusted lawyer.** Find someone with experience working with foreign buyers.

- **Budget for more than just the purchase price.** Old buildings might be cheap but restoring them isn't.

- **Local connections are key.** 'Bring someone you trust – who speaks the local language fluently – to meetings, especially in traditional communities where a male companion might help smooth the way.'

- **Prepare for bureaucracy.** 'There's a lot of paperwork, so be patient – it's all part of the process.'

Desiree Prinsloo is an award-winning artist who divides her time between Sydney and Hydra, drawing inspiration from the island's beauty. Desiree shares her passion through art workshops and retreats on Hydra.

A Travel Life in Style

Adventure can also be found even as responsibilities mount. Sydney stylist Ainslie Curran weaves wanderlust through school pickups and business meetings, fashion buying trips and family travels – a reminder that with enough determination and planning, the explorer's spirit can thrive in any circumstance.

The bell tinkles as I push open the door to Ainslie's boutique, sunlight streaming through the windows and dancing off the rails of her carefully curated collection. She's adjusting a display of dresses – each one telling a story of her travels, from hand-made pieces in the small Italian villages to Parisian ateliers.

'Perfect timing,' she calls out, holding up a kaftan, handstitched in glorious-coloured thread. 'This one just arrived. Very you.' She's right, of course. After decades in fashion and beauty, working with giants like Giorgio Armani and Mecca Cosmetica, Ainslie has an eye that's intuitive. But it's her talent for weaving travel into the fabric of life that I find most fascinating.

'Remember when we used to just pack up and go?' she laughs, reminiscing about her pre-kids adventures. As a single mum to two teenage daughters, she still travels, just differently. Her secret? Lists. Lots of them. 'Sometimes I plan things right down to the hour,' she admits, pulling out her phone to show me her meticulously organised calendar. It's this fastidious planning that allows her to squeeze in annual fashion buying trips while running her boutique and raising her daughters. 'I thrive on the energy and adventure,' she says, 'but making it all work takes strategy.' This includes surrounding herself with trustworthy staff, outsourcing home duties when finances permit, and – perhaps most crucially – learning to let go. 'You can't do it all yourself,' she says wisely. 'And if something does fall over, it's not the end of the world. There's always tomorrow.'

Her daughters have become seasoned travellers in their own right, accompanying her everywhere. 'They're brilliant explorers, and honestly, they often know better than me what's new and where to go.' Ainslie has developed a unique approach to family travel planning. 'For the month before any trip, we have a weekly dinner where everyone – including me – brings new and interesting suggestions to the table. We skip the tourist traps, preferring to get amongst the locals, eat where they eat, stay in boutique hotels. It brings so much more to our travels.'

But perhaps the most significant shift in Ainslie's journey has been her approach to wellbeing. 'For years, everyone came before me,' she reflects. 'I lived on a poor diet and stress, like so many women do. But as I've aged, I've realised that life is about what you put into yourself first – everyone else's happiness follows.'

Now, hot yoga sessions clear her head and weekly personal training builds the strength needed for long buying trips and marathon styling sessions. A naturopath has transformed her approach to nutrition.

As we wrap up our chat, a customer calls for her attention. Before heading over, she turns back with a smile. 'Travel, family, business, wellbeing – you can have it all. Perhaps, as they say, not all at once – just be clever about how you piece it together.'

Ainslie Curran is a Sydney stylist known for transforming spaces with creativity. With over two decades of experience in fashion and beauty, Ainslie also owns the renowned boutique LoveDuck in Paddington.

Conquering Fear, One Stroke at a Time

Marie-Therese Hunter and I connect over the phone from her home in Western Australia. Her warm voice belies the steely determination that once propelled her through a gruelling 19.2 km solo Rottnest Channel swim. But there's more to Marie-Therese than her aquatic achievements – her journey from sleep scientist to endurance athlete is a testament to the power of mid-life reinvention.

'What was the catalyst?' I ask.

'Approaching 40, I felt this urge to do something just for me. I'd seen car licence plates around Perth given to swimmers who completed this event, and I thought, *I want one of those.*'

She emphasises her journey wasn't just about physical endurance; it was a profound lesson in overcoming fear. 'The day of the swim, conditions were terrible. My husband dropped me off, saying, 'No-one will think less of you if you don't complete it' – those words lit a fire in me.'

As she recounts battling treacherous waters, I'm struck by her resilience. 'It wasn't about the number plate anymore,' she says. 'It became about the people supporting me – my brother stepping in as paddler, the skipper, my husband. I realised it was a team effort, even in a solo swim.'

'How has this experience shaped your approach to fear in other areas of life?' I probe.

'Fear motivates me now. I take ownership of it, analyse it, then plan to overcome it. Whether it's open water swimming or travelling solo at 50, I've learned to use fear as a catalyst for growth.' I asked her for advice, how to balance time out versus family life.

'Balance is elusive,' she admits. 'No-one I know has truly mastered it. Now, in mid-life, with my career winding down and my personal passions taking shape, it's all new territory. What helps me is talking to close female friends, seeking their wisdom when I feel stretched thin. And with my husband and family, it's about honest communication. Letting them know what I need creates a space where love and understanding can grow, and that's where the balance starts to find its way. You can also bring them along for the journey,' she adds. 'More recent endeavours have become a family affair – one of my children cycled with me on a charity ride while the other volunteered. Further opportunities to make a difference and bring people together.'

Marie-Therese Hunter is a clinical neurophysiology scientist, accomplished distance swimmer, martial artist, and advocate for physical fitness. She inspires others to confront fear and pursue adventures with determination and resilience.

Eat, Pray, Love ... and Launch a Business

Several years ago, Aisha Hilary-Morgan left behind a 15-year corporate career for 105 days of solo travel across 50 destinations – I had many questions, so I knew we needed to speak.

Our phone chat from her home in Singapore begins with the expected, 'What prompted such a drastic change?'

'I was burnt out, bound by expectations,' she recalls. 'One day, I just snapped. I left my job and my understanding husband for what became my Eat, Pray, Love experience.'

Recalling my own decision to embark on a solo adventure, I ask, 'How did your husband react to this decision?'

His response was a selfless act of love, she acknowledges. 'His only request was that we reunite every six weeks for the 'love' part of the journey – reunions which strengthened our bond.' This echoes recent research on relationships showing that solo travel can enhance relationship satisfaction, particularly when partners support each other's individual growth.

'Can you share some highlights from your 105-day journey?' I ask, eager to hear about the diverse experiences that shaped her transformation.

'From the vibrant streets of India to the tranquil landscapes of Laos, each destination offered a new lesson,' Aisha says, the excitement evident in her voice. 'A highlight was in Nepal. I found myself having breakfast with a local family and washing their elephants – those serendipitous moments you can never plan for.'

'How did these experiences shape your return to 'normal' life?' I ask.

'Everything changed. My mantra became 'What's next?' I learned to trust my instincts, find joy in uncertainty. When I returned, I couldn't go back to corporate life. Instead, I launched a business.' Her words resonate, reminding me of my own post-travel entrepreneurial endeavours.

Rediscovering what was important in life led Aisha to start her business Hills & West Interiors and Accessories.

'What advice would you give to other women considering a similar journey?'

Aisha pauses. 'Dream big and write down your deepest desires. Embrace connection with all kinds of people. Lean into uncertainty – it's where the magic happens. And most importantly, love yourself first. It's not selfish; it's essential.'

After 15 years in the corporate world, Aisha Hillary-Morgan founded Hills & West following a life-changing journey across 50 destinations. She encourages women to embrace uncertainty, pursue passions and prioritise self-love to realise their dreams.

Walking Towards Self-Discovery

As the founder of Filipino Food Movement Australia and the creative force behind Adobo Down Under, Anna Manlulo's journey from culinary ambassador to long-distance pilgrim intrigues me.

'Anna, what made you decide to embark on the Camino after years of dreaming about it?' I ask, curious about the timing of her decision.

She laughs. 'A combination of things. My kids were older, more independent. Then a friend completed the full 720 km walk, and I thought, *If not now, when?* As a Catholic, the Camino held spiritual significance for me, but it was also about searching for answers.' As she describes the moment she committed to the journey, I'm reminded of the power of seizing opportunities.

'How did the reality of the Camino compare to your expectations?' I inquire.

'It was so much more than I imagined. The physical challenge was one thing, but the mental and spiritual aspects ... those were transformative.'

She paints a vivid picture of her days on the Camino – the pre-dawn starts, the simple routines, the camaraderie among pilgrims. 'We'd wake at 5:30 am, walk, eat, do laundry, sleep, and repeat. I lived with two sets of clothes, basic toiletries, and learned to sleep in rooms with 30-plus other people. There were moments of doubt,' she admits. 'But then I'd notice something small – the muddy ground, the green moss, the sound of cowbells – and I'd be anchored back in the present.'

'How did your background in food and culture influence your Camino experience?' I ask, knowing her passion for culinary traditions.

Anna chuckles. 'Oh, it definitely played a part! I walked 315 km over 15 days, and along the way, I ate and drank my way through the Castilla y Leon and Galicia regions. After the Camino, I went on a gastronomic tour of Spain. It was a beautiful way to connect my love for food with this spiritual journey.'

'What lessons did you bring back from the Camino?' I ask.

Anna pauses, thoughtful. 'That every day is an opportunity for learning and growth. And that it's up to me to fill my own cup. The Camino taught me that travelling solo isn't as scary as I thought – it's empowering.'

Anna Manlulo, founder of the Filipino Food Movement Australia, is a passionate cook and writer. She promotes Filipino culinary culture through her social channels, Adobo Down Under. Anna is now working on a cookbook celebrating Filipino cuisine.

The Art of Creativity

Everyone has a story; the air is full of stories. The creative process is mysterious, I don't know why it is that suddenly a theme will take hold of me and refuse to leave me in peace until I investigate it and write it.

– Isabel Allende

You don't need a specific space (or equipment). Some of my BEST writing has been done in my head – perhaps captured, perhaps not – but oh, the joy of letting your imagination roam free.

In mid-life, writing has been a saviour, a private constant during times of despair.

You never need explain yourself to your jottings, you just start tapping (or pick up the pen) and venture into a world of creation. Since I first held a pencil, I've written – short stories, diary notes, letters to pen pals. I initially didn't identify as a 'writer' – it was just how I made sense of the world, putting it to words. One day, I heard of this new thing called 'blogging', tentatively beginning to put my words 'out there'. At some point along the way, buoyed by a small but steady following of my musings, I decided to up the stakes and go 'study the craft'. The two-year fiction writing school was an invaluable learning ground: how to structure a story, develop character, plot. There are three novels that will never see the light of day but were 'therapy' in the early days of mothering overwhelm. Knowing I was drawn to telling 'real stories', a friend directed me to the Australian Writers Centre – several courses,

My youngest has a gift with words, and finds putting thoughts and feelings on the page is a positive antidote to an online world.

Research on the therapeutic benefits of writing find it can significantly reduce symptoms of anxiety, particularly in individuals processing traumatic experiences.

265

and dozens of article rejections later, I landed a contributing editor role in a national magazine.

For you, it might be painting, cooking, reading another's words. You may not see yourself as 'creative' at all. My husband, a financial whiz, would never consider he had a proclivity for right-brain pursuits, yet I've seen him in rapture at art galleries and producing Excel spreadsheets of such linear form and pattern they ARE an artform.

For what is making art, and who are you doing it for? I'd suggest yourself as a start, and if you feel drawn to sharing – well, you must never stifle that urge. There is space for us all to develop a ritual of learning more about ourselves through creating art.

A recurring theme you will have now noted – eventually, perseverance pays off.

Writing Through Grief

Virginia Lloyd – author, book coach, and publishing consultant – and I first crossed paths when I was seeking guidance on writing this book.

Discovering her work with famed author Lily Brett almost stopped me from making contact – employing 'why not now' gave me the nudge.

Her tale, turning personal tragedy into creative expression, is both heartbreaking and inspiring.

'Virginia, your story for our conversation begins with an unimaginable loss. How did writing become a part of your healing process?'

'When I was widowed at the age of 34, I immediately felt so much older than my peers. Instead of focusing on career goals, dating, or starting a family, I faced endless financial and bureaucratic questions relating to my husband John that felt intrusive and disrespectful. My family and close friends were supportive and attentive, but I was isolated in overwhelming grief. Almost immediately, I understood that not only had my life changed forever; I had too.

'About 18 months after John died, I rented out my house and moved to New York. I'd always loved the city and had wanted to live there for a while, so it felt more like a gap year than anything longer. In my widowhood, I couldn't see or think further ahead than that. Fragile but hopeful, I landed in New York and joined a playwriting class to do something with all the emotional baggage I'd lugged with me. What began as a play ended up as my first book, *The Young Widow's Book of Home Improvement*.

'In Sydney, I'd worked as a book editor, so I had always been tough on my own scribble. But now, broken open, my attitude in writing the earliest drafts was simply to let my thoughts fall to the page. Some part of me knew that it would be valuable to capture all the taboo, irreverent, incongruous, and downright silly things that I'd felt and thought but had kept to myself. I learned there's a marathon of revision between those initial sentences and a crafted manuscript, but if you're compelled to write about a life-changing experience then you must start by getting all of it out of your head and down on the page.

'My gap year became permanent, and almost 20 years later, I still live in New York. Reflecting on the process of writing my first book, it's clear that what I most needed was solitude and mental space more than a specific location. Getting away will look different for everyone, but it could be as local as making over an empty-nest bedroom into a writing den, joining a class, and turning up to every meeting or as exotic as travelling to a dedicated writers' retreat to kick-start your writing project. The important thing is not to worry about the quality or end result of your efforts. By freeing your brain of the immediate thoughts and memories, you will find you can go deeper into the material that lies beyond. As a wonderful writing teacher once told me, there's news that only you can bring.'

Virginia Lloyd is an author, book coach, and publishing consultant who transformed personal tragedy into creative expression after being widowed at 34. With decades of literary experience, she helps writers find their voice and navigate publishing.

Ideas for a Grown Up's Gap Year

'Life List', 'Bucket List', 'Take A Break List' – you choose the header, then go wild with possibility. Begin with 'if time and money were no object' then whittle it down to 'conceivably doable for me' – while some of the former may remain, the latter are where the golden ticket to time-out may lie. While you mull your options, start a Pinterest folder with destinations and activities that appeal. I also like to visit second-hand bookstores for travel guides – in the beginning of research mode, it doesn't matter if some of the finer details are outdated.

What You Tell Me

A question I asked on social media – 'Where do you escape close to home when you need a moment?' – resulted in responses flooding in.

Essentially to reassure myself I am 'not the only one' ....

'I take a tent and drive to a camping ground on the sea – just an hour from home, just one night watching the stars and reading.'

'I hike, under the guise of training for a charity event (which I am) but not entirely altruistic – if I announced a full day out to go to the beauty salon, that wouldn't wash so well on the home front. So this way, I'm alone on the coastal track, exercising in nature, and doing something nice for someone else. Win-win. 'Running away lite', I call it.'

'Three girlfriends and I started a tradition when our babies were young – taking two nights away. One of us has a family shack, so it is same place, same time, every year. We divvy up the prep (one shops, one does dinner, one cleans, one drives) – when we arrive, we can forget making decisions. It's our sacred time to be alone together.'

'A facial. When I need a moment, I book a facial – 90 minutes, because one hour is NOT long enough to chill. Salon policy means my phone has to be off (I let only my mum know, just in case there is an emergency with the kids). I look for opening specials at new locations each time – keeps it fresh and in my budget.'

Wonderful escapes can come in surprising packages. One early December, pre-exams season madness when the boys were little, I camped out at Mum's coastal abode for five nights. Being mothered in your fifties is just as nice as it was at age 5. We walked, we talked, we went out for an 'adults' dinner. Another time, I stumbled upon a 'retreat' special an hour from home – spending a weekend sleeping in a single bed, in a room with 'barely enough space to turn around'. I hadn't slept so restfully for decades.

These trips taught me that 'away' is more a state of mind than a GPS coordinate. A sense of 'newness', change of scenery and a fresh perspective – even if that perspective is simply remembering what it's like to have someone else make the bed.

Closer to Home

Home sanctuary. Sometimes, we cannot get away, or don't want to. Maybe we've spent effort and money creating our sanctuary and then become so busy we barely have time to relax in our carefully curated space. If you live in a full household – try to farm out your crew and enjoy your own space in peace. Don't answer the phone. Don't make plans (except booking a few local treatments). Use the time to journal, stroll, deliberate, sleep, breathe, clean up your nutrition, or be in nature.

Use what you have. Investigate what modalities your health fund covers. Try new options such as acupuncture, herbal medicine, traditional medicine, massage, ayurvedic, or facial massage.

Upskill. Local classes; cooking a style of cuisine you'd never considered, such as plant-based, Vietnamese, or *shojin ryori*; new practices such as meditation and mindfulness groups or yoga teaching.

Start a group. They say that great things happen when like-minded people come together. Take inspiration from the Monday Morning Cooking Club. What began as a casual gathering of six

Jewish women has grown into a sisterhood that spans the globe. These women meet every Monday to cook, share stories, and celebrate their heritage through food. But it's more than just a cooking club – it's a support system, a creative outlet, and a way to give back to the community through charity work.

Further Away

Longer term, local life. Live like a local in a place you've always dreamt of calling home. Immerse yourself in the culture, savour the local cuisine, and make meaningful connections. **TRY THIS.** Housesitting is an interesting option, enabling you to enjoy an extended stay.

Founder Chip Conley recently authored Learning to Love Midlife: 12 Reasons Why Life Gets Better with Age.

Study break. Is there a subject you've always been curious about? Lifelong learning may well slow cognitive and memory decline as we age – sign me up. **TRY THIS.** Contact local organisations in your area of interest; they may have affiliations interstate or overseas (e.g., if ceramics are your thing – investigate areas in Japan with homestay and local craft study opportunities). Modern Elder Academy, based in North America, might call to you with their curriculum focused entirely on living a more fulfilling mid-life.

Volunteer work. Teach English to Buddhist monks in Thailand, care for baby sea turtles in the Whitsundays, or help in disaster areas. Become involved on a regular basis within your community or make it part of a longer break. Be mindful of actually contributing to a project and not simply filling a gap that is taking work from a local person (a building project might seem well and good; however, some international volunteer groups are doing work a local builder might have).

TRY THIS

Red Cross are apolitical, with domestic and international opportunities; Earthwatch have a register of scientists looking for assistance.

Adventure. Explore rugged terrains, hike in exotic jungles, or embark on a cross-country road trip. Adventure travel can push you out of your comfort zone and provide life-changing experiences.

Say Yes 52 Times

Celebrate a bit of novelty with verve and an intentional kind of determination. This idea is not unique, but definitely fun. Brainstorm and write down a list of 52 things to say yes to this year. This could include trying a new cuisine each week, attending local community events, saying thank you to someone who shaped you, learning a new skill through online tutorials, or volunteering for different causes. Keep this list visible and check off each item as you go, celebrating the small but significant ways you're enriching your life.

Get it? 52 weeks – A Grown Up's Gap Year

Now, go forth and create your own Grown Up's Gap Year novelty. Whether it's a series of mini-adventures or grand escapades – the most important thing is to start. As philosopher and writer Lao Tzu said, 'The journey of a thousand miles begins with one step.'

So, what will your first step be?

Breakout: Leaving Room for Serendipity

Author Pico Iyer says, 'We travel, initially, to lose ourselves; and we travel next to find ourselves.' His words echoed what I'd started to discover – beauty found in leaving space for the unknown. But life being life, we've discussed the practicality of upping sticks and taking off without notice would rock any home front – dependents, spouse, work, bills – there is no doubt you will have to instigate some 'plans'. Also be prepared to leave yourself room to wing it – do not over-engineer. Leaving space for discovery should be the point of all this.

Research shows that people with an open mindset and positive mood are more likely to notice and act on chance opportunities, fostering serendipity in their lives.

As I felt more open, I've since logged on to random online weekend courses to find a woman on Zoom who was at my primary school – in another country. In Zurich, an Insta-friend recognised my kaftan in the lounge. Not 24 hours later I was dining in a Venetian palazzo – mid-summer fireball sun setting over the Grand Canal – at the home of 'Mimi'. A chance reintroduction 43 years after I admired her kaftan as a 12-year-old around a pool in Fiji. On and on – enough happy accidents to fill another book.

'Serendipity' comes from a 1557 Persian fairytale, *The Three Princes of Serendip*, about princes who made unexpected discoveries.

Leave space for your own synchronicities and send me a note to tell me about them. I live for these stories!

Expert: Lisa Manser – the Heart of Retreat Philosophy

Lisa Manser knows well how we might feel restored – after all, it is her business. As COMO Shambhala Global Spa and Wellness Director, Lisa is responsible for designing some of the world's most luxurious protocols and treatments. Her mission? To educate and empower guests to discover optimal wellbeing.

During our conversation, we explore our synergistic relationship with daily wellness rituals (rising early, in gratitude is where we both begin). I also learn plenty (going upside down to invigorate is where you might now find me), and what COMO sees as the future of optimising individual wellness.

MvT: 'Let's begin with what wellbeing means to you, Lisa.'

Lisa: 'A riff on wellbeing becomes 'being well' – a goal that looks different for all. Wellbeing is so much more than do or don't do. I prefer not to fixate on a destination, but rather see each step along the path as trialling what moves you closer to feeling stronger, healthier, more peaceful, and more joyful. Not just eating this and that, or moving a prescriptive way, sleeping a fixed number of hours. Those pillars of health are important; however, it is also using intentional words, eliminating negative low-vibrating vocabulary – choosing positivity, fun, joy, spirituality, and connection. These are the heart of wellbeing for me.

'As our world increasingly speeds up it becomes harder to maintain healthful practices – our brain is hardwired to take the easiest route, the path of least resistance – so in order to be intentional and purposeful, we need to 'create a new pathway in the brain'. As you discussed, it takes time for the brain to say yes to change. Many of life's answers come when you retreat, even if just for a moment each day.'

MvT: 'How do you deliver wellbeing for guests at COMO Shambhala?'

Lisa: 'Our environment plays a significant part – although boasting the best beach or the 'in' place to be seen holds little interest. Instead, we focus on local surroundings subtly seeping into the environs, understated beauty rather than the obvious.

'It is the seemingly small detail where we shine for guests, the spaces we leave bare intentionally so your senses can rest and reset. I recently designed holistic 'wellness paths' tailored to an individual by a dedicated consultant. Guests might arrive with an intention, maybe wanting to detox, but a stressed system is detected – therapists guide them through a plan where they will see better results and ultimately feel better. This way of guiding wellness resides firmly in our ethos.'

MvT: 'How do you encourage guests to follow through on an intention to continue the retreat learnings when they return home, when life might take over?'

Lisa: 'We guide a lifestyle, not just a one-and-done spa retreat. This is why our guests return – we offer many options to bring what they learn with us home, so when they return, we can build on this base.

'It is learning to listen to your body to nourish it best. COMO's philosophy – 'choose wisely for your body, choose what makes you feel good' – extends to what we eat. The COMO Shambhala Kitchen offers delicious nurturing food and sends guests home with a favourite dish to recreate from our cookbook *The Pleasures of Eating Well*. But really, the essence comes via COMO Hotels and Resorts visionary founder, Christina Ong, who cites 'wellness begins within'. We get to choose 'life'; how we move through each day, and how we interact with fellow humans and bring joy to someone else. The ripple-on effect costs nothing except empathy. A heartfelt 'thank you, I see you, I appreciate you, you are doing an amazing job' is all it takes to connect. Never underestimate this simple yet powerful way to change the whole dynamic and vibration of your life and for others.'

Retreat at Home: Creating Your Own Regime

TRY THIS

MvT: 'My readers may be surprised to learn it is a pared-back aesthetic you incorporate into your own daily wellness practices.'

Lisa: 'A blend of innovation and traditional wisdom – intent and purpose as my guide, not perfection. For a sustainable way to approach feeling better in mind and body, I focus on:

1. Waking with the sunrise every morning.

2. A moment of gratitude for another day, through intention and purpose. Not simply platitudes – lying still immersed in a sense of being in the moment.

3. A moment of journalling – about the day before, what could be done better today.

4. Daily spiritual practice.

5. I begin by turning the day on its head; a forward bend, downward dog, or headstand – if inversion is not for you, an invigorating (self) head massage. Delivering oxygen-rich blood to the brain and removing toxins is key.

6. Movement, every day; walk, gym, dance, and stretch.

7. A morning 'health' shake; ingredients might include a mushroom blend, turmeric, red rice yeast, walnuts, and

spirulina – all among the building blocks for a stronger constitution.

8. Organic food, as much as possible.

9. A great 'hairdo' does wonders too!

10. Taking time to let the mind wander to give my brain a break.'

Lisa Jody Manser is a wellness strategist with over 15 years of experience developing wellness programs for prestigious luxury spas, wellness resorts, and clients worldwide. She specialises in wellness integration, nutrition, movement, and lifestyle coaching, driving transformative wellness experiences globally. Her studies in wellness coaching and naturopathy reinforce her passion for holistic wellbeing.

Why I Am a Fan of Best-Practice Wellbeing Retreats

There's a reason the notion of 'taking the waters' has existed for centuries. Long before wellness became a trillion-dollar industry, humans understood the profound healing power of intentional retreat. Joining a structured retreat, whether it's a wellness retreat, a creative writing retreat, or a spiritual retreat, can be a transformative experience. When facilitated properly, it is the most cosseted feeling, akin to being cared for like a child again – to have most decisions made for you, from nutrition to activity and limited exposure to the outside world. The ultimate in letting go.

A gold standard retreat? I place emphasis on sophisticated simplicity: farm-to-table nutrition, just enough 'ommm' to replenish 'oomph', and considered wellbeing treatments that deliver results beyond mere pampering. I purposely look for 'off the well-trod path', wishing to immerse myself in local experiences. I may initially rail against 'getting out of my comfort zone'; however, it is precisely this feeling I come for.

A Grown Up's Gap Year Diary Note ...

I arrive in the small village late Saturday afternoon, everything closed. Low-grade panic sets in. What on earth have I committed to? Traversing three countries to thrust myself into the extreme depths of countryside Austria. I've loved the buzz of seaside 'Euro summer', juxtaposed with French Alpine life – je ne sais quoi *coursing through both.*

The hotel is quiet, just the tinkle of teacups from a table of three ruddy-faced women – hiking sticks propped against their chairs. The receptionist walks me along silent corridors to my room, home for the next 10 days – the room sparse. Everything I need and nothing more. Fitting. I fling open my balcony door – letting in crisp air. The scent of cow dung wafts in on the breeze.

Here, rural life is life. The next morning, on an early hike, tomato-red tractors stand out against the green – mountains, grass, shutters.

Returning to the hotel, I pass the fitness room, where a beaming young man pokes his head out and hands me a set of headphones, motioning me in – the space full of healthy folk of all generations, bound by vitality. 'Feel the energy …,' he chants. Rather than sounding like psychobabble, it motivates. Releases the beast, as it were. Just what I need – a sanctuary far from my comfort zone, miles from familiarity, forcing me to look within. Surrender to the moment. By day three, the cow manure doesn't smell like poo; it smells organic. By day 10, I'm looking at my diary to see the earliest moment I can return.

Remember 'the picture' we stuck on our mirror earlier? My picture was Hotel Post Bezau – a dream realised.

Healing History of Retreats

The Romans built elaborate thermal complexes for cleansing, restoration, and social connection. These were not simply 'pampering palaces', either; many were prescriptive spaces where physicians like Galen would recommend specific bathing rituals and treatments for various ailments. They were early pioneers of what we now call integrative wellness, combining thermal therapies with strict dietary regimens and exercise in nature. Many of their

Research validates what the ancients intuited – that structured retreat experiences can reduce cortisol levels by up to 40% within just three days.

281

methodologies – from lymphatic drainage to hydrotherapy – remain cornerstone treatments in modern medical spas.

Different Paths to Retreat

Medical spa retreats. A stalwart of European wellness tradition, with a range of therapies and treatments overseen by medical professionals. Often specialising in anti-ageing and detox programs.

Yoga retreats. If you're looking to deepen your yoga practice, Rishikesh in India, known as the birthplace of yoga, offers a spiritual and immersive experience. Bali, Indonesia, is another hotspot, with its lush landscapes and serene atmosphere. Perhaps Ubud (hello, *Eat, Pray, Love*) for a holistic yoga retreat. In Australia, Byron Bay.

Health and wellness retreats. For comprehensive wellbeing, health and wellness retreats focus on nutrition, fitness, mindfulness, and mental health, from transformative weight-loss and detox programs to holistic wellness programs that address emotional and spiritual wellbeing.

Luxury retreats. Upscale retreats work hard to instil transformation that can be brought home – 'preventative wellness', as COMO Hotels and Resorts and Six Senses Kyoto show us.

Cultural Retreat Philosophy

An introduction via a mutual friend is how Ayako Fukuda, Director of Wellness at Six Senses Kyoto, and I become acquainted. Ayako glows with good health and zen – the embodiment of wellbeing we might all hope to sustain from a retreat in one of the most beautiful and historic cities in the world.

Solo Trip Diary Note …

Ten solitary days in Kyoto, Japan, an experience immersed in ancient tradition, with nature omnipresent. Even in the city centre, you don't need to go far to find tranquillity; if you come prepared to wander, you will be rewarded with small lanes leading away from the throngs on shopping streets, the popular food markets, the 'must see' sites. An early morning walk to Kiyomizu-dera Buddhist Temple yields only a few other bodies (the early hour and a wintery chill keep the crowds at bay). Keep walking behind the temple grounds and you will come to an all but deserted road leading up the hill to yet another temple. I sit and meditate on the peace and quiet that belies the unmistakable fact that Kyoto remains one of the most visited cities in the world – proof that ZEN can be found almost anywhere if you are prepared to be still for a moment.

'What does wellbeing mean to you?' I ask Ayako, curious about the philosophy behind this luxury retreat.

'Culturally (in Japan), we have several versions of wellbeing – one thought is happiness, and of course we are familiar with the word *ikigai*, the sense of living a life filled with purpose and joy. For our culture, wellbeing is not simply a trip to the spa, rather how the person can feel better as a whole.'

Echoing Lisa Manser's sentiments.

Ayako explains how treatments at Six Senses are designed to align with nature's rhythms, helping guests find balance with the changing seasons. 'We believe that true wellbeing begins with restoring balance between humanity, the earth, and the heavens, and being mindful of the moment that you are in.'

As our chat winds down, I'm struck by how Six Senses Kyoto has managed to blend ancient Japanese wellness concepts with modern luxury, creating an experience that doesn't end when you check out. It's a philosophy of wellness that travels with you, transforming a retreat stay into a lifelong journey of wellbeing.

Ayako Fukuda holds a master's degree in acupuncture and brings over a decade of holistic wellness experience to her role as Director of Wellness at Six Senses Kyoto, curating transformative experiences that nurture the body, mind, and spirit.

Nature retreats. Retreats in stunning landscapes offer rejuvenation through physical immersion, an ice bathing retreat next on my list. Aro Hā Wellness Retreat in New Zealand's Southern Alps offers an immersive experience in nature, with hiking, yoga, and plant-based cuisine.

Spiritual retreats. For those seeking a deeper spiritual connection, spiritual retreats are ideal. Japan offers a host of temple lodgings amid pilgrimage trails. Ditto the Camino, as Anna wrote about in a previous chapter.

Silent retreats. Also known as 'silent fasting'. For those seeking inner peace through silence, silent retreats provide an opportunity to disconnect from the noise of the world.

When my friend M called to ask if I was including commentary on silent retreats in my book, I had to admit it wasn't on my radar. My idea of taking off solo was rooted in rediscovery through interactions with others. A little time spent 'sitting with my thoughts' was one thing, but four days without talking? No, thank you.

'You might actually enjoy it,' M said, a mischievous lilt in her voice. 'It's an adventure, and you know well that adventures come in many forms. It's a challenge, and it's incredibly rewarding.'

M shared her experience of leaving behind a life of constant motion for days of silence. Initially, the quiet was deafening, but as days passed, she found herself slipping into a rhythm of being more present. 'When everything is quiet, the most happens,' wrote Danish philosopher Søren Kierkegaard. M discovered just how true this is.

She left the retreat carrying with her the ability to create pockets of silence amidst the chaos of everyday life (echoing Kate Kendall's earlier story). My verdict? I'm not ruling out an adventure into silence. After all, there's a certain allure to the idea of finding peace – not by escaping, but by embracing the quiet that's always been there, waiting to be heard.

TRY THIS

If I asked you to close your eyes and think about a place where you might find restoration, calm, joy – where comes into your mind? Write that spot down (and if it is really lofty, whic is perfectly fine, add a spot 'more likely' in the interim). Sign up for websites to hear about retreats in these places and seasonal specials – this helps to feel that it is within your grasp. If not now, then at the right time. Research thoroughly, read reviews – I also ask what 'take-home' programs are included. Too often, I observe guests struggling with how the in-house lifestyle shifts translate into their home worlds.

Breakout

Heed This: Do Not Become 'Trapped by Treatments'

Like many, I had always assumed a packed schedule of spa treatments would leave me feeling blissfully renewed. But as a *Vogue* magazine's article on the 'wellness trap' highlights, mirroring my own experience, sometimes less is more.

A Grown Up's Gap Year Diary Note …

A small posse of us gather each day after yoga to swap local tips and spa stories. A woman from Belgium, mid-thirties, nursing a broken heart. A regular retreat visitor to escape stress, yet she confesses, 'I'm stressed!' She has booked herself solid with treatments and now all she wants is to flop by the pool with a book.

'Trapped by treatments,' I quip. And just like that, our cautionary in-joke is born – one I ignore at my peril.

It's my last 24 hours in the Austrian alps, and suddenly I'm possessed by the spirit of FOMO, wanting to do whatever I can to pursue and prolong the feeling of wellbeing. I sign up for everything, including qi gong *with a portly Slovakian gentleman. He delivers the entire class in German, blissfully unaware that I don't understand a word. Next, a massage with a firm-handed Swiss physio, who hits every ticklish spot on my body, making it a challenge to stifle laughter. Then a lymphatic drainage facial – soft touch, a bit weird, but surprisingly relaxing. The grand finale? A 'sauna and essence' session with the rotund* qi gong *master. Swimwear in European saunas* verboten, *his modesty towel threatens to abandon ship with each vigorous towel wave. As he cranks up the heat, I dream of escaping to the cooling brine pool just visible through the heat haze. Then, with one final hefty wave, his cover slips a bit further, and I lose it. I'm out of there, howling with laughter and definitely ruining the zen. My tip? Don't chase your tail ticking off the wellness boxes – explore, experiment, but don't get lured into being so busy 'trapped by treatments' that a retreat stay becomes more racing, less contemplating your naval.*

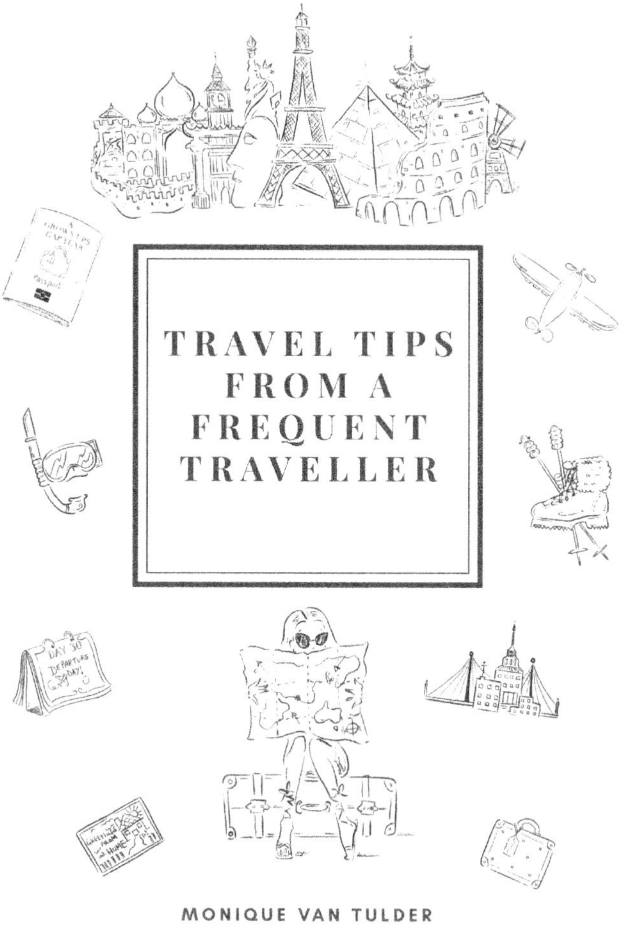

TRAVEL TIPS FROM A FREQUENT TRAVELLER

MONIQUE VAN TULDER

All my travel tips in a free travel guide available through clicking on the QR code:

SUMMER POSSIBILITIES

As you conclude the 'Summer – Feel Adventurous' section, we covered a lot of ground during this vibrant season. Here's how the chapters guide you towards embracing freedom, adventure, and self-discovery:

1. **Embracing freedom of exploration.** Whether solo or with friends, reflect on the transformative power of travel to inspire your version of adventure.

   ### TRY THIS

   Plan a short solo getaway – a night away or an afternoon to yourself. Permission to recharge, alone.

2. **Discovering the philosophy of retreats.** Learn how to infuse regimes from best-practice wellness retreats into your lifestyle.

   ### TRY THIS

   Dedicate an afternoon to mimic a wellness retreat – start with a 20-minute mindful walk, prepare a seasonal, plant-based meal, and finish with a tech-free evening and yin yoga or stretching before bed.

3. **Adventure as a healing journey.** Recognise that adventure can be more than just excitement – it can be a path to healing.

Expand your horizons through walking, writing, or simply answering the call of nature.

TRY THIS

Carry a journal with you on your adventures. Write down your thoughts and experiences as they happen and reflect on how they make you feel.

4. **Pick adventure.** Whether you're planning a grand adventure or a simple getaway, preparation will help you make the most of your experiences.

TRY THIS

Engage in an outdoor activity that excites you, such as hiking, kayaking, or ocean swimming. Aim for one adventure each week.

5. **Live in the moment.** Learn to leave space for unexpected joys and embrace the serendipitous moments.

TRY THIS

Practise trusting your instincts. Whether in decision-making or choosing your next adventure, lean to the voice that guides your heart.

Summer is a season of exhilaration and limitless possibilities. Use this time to fuel your spirit with adventure and enrich your life with new experiences.

AUTUMN
FEEL CONNECTED

Time to take your reinvigorated self and incorporate it back into your life – with boundaries in place – enjoy a simplified, curated lifestyle with a sense of being connected to self. Project you has evolved into a solid design (ready to change as your future does). Go forth joyful seeking.

Practically speaking, Autumn is the season to:

1. Feel connected with your later-in-life tribe.

2. Repurpose a career or take a new step; discover how you are going to use your time.

3. Consolidate your new design for an interesting life. Enjoy love in all its guises.

4. Reconfirm where the treasure lies in your life.

Returning Home

Remember, 'No-one's more important than people'! In other words
friendship is the most important thing – not career or housework, o
one's fatigue – and it needs to be tended and nurtured.

– Julia Child, My Life in France

Life cannot be sustained on 'holiday feels' alone. A thriving human
requires more in the tank than pina coladas and pretty sunsets
Then again, freedom once sampled – at a slow and purposefu
pace – is intoxicating. Post-trip blues are a very real phenomenon

A Grown Up's Gap Year Diary Note (reflection upon return to th
marital home) …

Was I glad to return? A loaded question that requires a delicate answer.

Yes, because I love my sons, husband, family, friends – they are home. No, because I love who I became – I was frightened she would be absorbed back into the fold and not heard from again.

I began to cross my fingers as 'home time' drew near – that is until I visited Victoria, the clairvoyant in a hippie shop.

'But what should I really do?' I implore her. 'With the rest of my life?'

'Stop looking to other places for the answers – you already have those,' she replied. Unprompted, she added, 'Your husband is the one,' looking at me over her glasses with a fixated stare.

Like old friends, the very best of family relationships can take a pause without the earth caving in – that is to say, take a breather, and we will be here when you come up for air. My husband, given to few words on the matter, showed his love by flying to meet me (halfway) on the return journey – possibly to make sure I actually made it back to Australian soil – but truly, it was his version of 'I love you and I am glad you came home'. My sons – well, they probably felt relief but expressed a sense of pride. One son was impressed that their mum 'had the balls to go looking for her answers' – (not that they don't expect to remain at the top of her 'people we love', but there is room for her to follow her dreams, too). A message for their own fulfilled and joy-filled futures. The other son said, 'I think you deserved it – time for yourself'. Frankly, these sentiments said more than a star-spangled welcome home party – I was precisely where I needed to be, with the people I wanted to be with.

Coming home isn't just about slotting back into place – it's abou holding onto the edges of who you've become. I wasn't going t let the boundaries I'd built dissolve into the folds of everyday lif And two years later? They haven't.

TRY THIS

Grab a copy of the classic *Jonathan Livingstc Seagull* – it's short, but it cuts deep. Lik Jonathan, maybe leaving your flock for moment is exactly what's needed to con back stronger, ready to fly higher on your own terms.

'Til Mid-Life Do Us Part, or Not

Long-term relationships are tricky – the ultimate marathon; comforting, frustrating, kind, boring, stifling, essential, loving, generous, precious, a privilege, lacking pizzaz (insert your descriptive). Default 'roles' settle after a period of time – they are hard to shift unless something else does.

Like one party running away, for example.

Maybe you and your partner feel like strangers after years of juggling family, careers, and the chaos of everyday life. Sometimes, it's about rekindling that connection; other times, it's about redefining what intimacy and partnership look like now that you're both different people. The journey doesn't end in mid-life – it just changes course.

Breakout

Love, in all its guises, can find us at any stage of life. Relationships evolve; some stay the course, some end, but that doesn't mean life can't yield a happy ending, leading to new, unexpected connections. My mother, for example, met her soulmate during an early morning beach swim – in her early seventies and far from feeling 'it was all over'.

Expert: Lissy Abrahams – From Drift to Greater Couple Depth in Mid-life

Lissy Abrahams, a psychotherapist with decades of experience, has spent her career helping couples rediscover each other in mid-life. She shares her advice:

'It's extremely common for partners to believe they know everything about each other when they've been together for a significant period. As a couples therapist, I can tell you it's not true! We can have parts of ourselves that we don't share with our partners. We often harbour secret hopes, dreams, and desires for our lives, adding to the lack of inspiration.

My therapy-shunning husband and I have made a pact to work our way through Lissy's questions – a fun and fresh experience for our relationship.

'So, what can you do? You can start by being curious about yourself and each other at this important stage. It's time to get to know each other again for who you are today. I suggest a series of conversations. Find a private setting where you can feel relaxed and give your full attention to each other. Start with one question [examples below], and listen fully to the answer without interrupting, showing interest in your partner's response. This is respectful. Only share your own reflections on the same question or topic so the conversation remains safe, mutual, and connected.'

Connection questions:

- How do you envision the next chapter of our life together?
- What's a dream or goal you've always wanted to pursue but haven't yet?
- What excites or worries you most about the next 5–10 years that we could address together?
- What's a way we can reignite fun and spontaneity in our relationship?
- What's a new activity we could try together to deepen our connection?
- What does intimacy look like to you at this stage in your life?

Lissy's insights aren't about grand gestures or sweeping changes. They're about small, intentional moments – questions asked over coffee, walks where real listening happens, and tiny shifts that reignite the connection. In mid-life, it's not about finding your way back to the beginning, but about discovering a new depth in the here and now. And that's a journey worth taking, together.

Lissy is a highly regarded psychotherapist and author, a therapist and lecturer at the prestigious Tavistock Relationships in London, founder of the therapy clinic Heath Group Practice, author of Relationship Reset *and the online program Fight Less, Love More, and podcast host of* Relationships Under the Microscope.

Goodbyes and All That Entails

Nothing truly prepares us for the heartbreak of losing someone close, whether through death or divorce. One of the hardest parts is letting go of the future we imagined with that person – the dreams we built together, now vanished in an instant. The quiet ache of adjusting to a new reality is something I've felt in my own life, from the passing of loved ones to the shattering aftermath of my parents' divorce (I was 21 and still feel the effects).

Grief often feels isolating, but as I've learned, strength can emerge from the darkest corners of life. Next, you'll hear a unique perspective on loss and resilience as I share a conversation that moved beyond everyday struggles to uncover how one woman found strength in the most difficult of circumstances.

The Strength We All Hold

I met Lisa Walker over a casual coffee, and what started as small talk quickly transformed into a deep conversation about loss, resilience, and the journey forward.

I'll let her tell her story.

'It's something we don't think too much about. Juggling, for women, is an inherent part of everyday life: kids, work, family, ourselves. We are often the bouncing board for ideas, for problems, and a vehicle for wisdom that is earned over a lifetime. I bet you don't even think about how strong you are. I didn't, until one day, at 47 years old, my husband Ben died suddenly. To say I was thrown into utter chaos is an understatement. I had to dig deep, find a new equilibrium, and locate a whole new inner strength I never knew existed.

'I needed to tell my two young boys that their father had passed away. Most possibly the worst moment of my life.

'And it doesn't end there; the realities of life do not stop to let you grieve. Managing finances, lawyers, paperwork. Bank accounts were frozen, a salary ended … the mortgage didn't. Somehow, I found the strength to negotiate and pull every lever to keep the wheels turning.

'As the dust settled, I felt the best way forward was a new space to begin our new version of 'family'. Change management is challenging: moving to a new neighbourhood, changing schools for very reluctant boys – all necessary steps – arduous by nature and all the more navigating it alone.

'And then, one year after Ben's passing, I made a decision. On my 49th birthday, I committed to my year of yes. Yes to joy, to life, to love, to friends, to experiences.

'Tears as I felt the ache of Ben not seeing the boys grow up.

'But also, yes to new beginnings.

'Yes is one word – but it brings so much power, positivity, strength and challenge. It has changed me, irrevocably for the better. Should you find yourself in a situation that seems insurmountable, the best advice I can offer is to follow what feels right for you, given your circumstances. As a grieving widow, starting a business might not have been the frequently traversed path, but what helped me heal was making a plan I felt was right for myself and my children. It gave me direction at a time I might have floundered. Only you will know the best way forward for you.' *Lisa Walker, co-founder of Eir Women, helps women over 40 unlock health and joy, blending her expertise in beauty marketing with personal experience to create solutions for mid-life women.*

Being Alone, but Not Necessarily Lonely

Silence can be golden and deafening in equal measure. A frantic life is exhausting until you don't have anything to hurry for – then it is exhausting to keep busy, find places to be, people to see. I've experienced both sides of the coin; living in a tiny bedsit as a young adult was a study in stoicism – new city, no money, no family, few friends, weekends that stretched an eternity after the first flush of exploration wore thin. I've also watched my mum (and dad) dive into 'alone time' post-divorce – moments of wobbles and wallowing, then getting on with getting on. And I've watched friends lose a spouse to death.

Choosing to live solo is entirely different from having it forced upon you. Both require planning and decision-making. The best advice from a long-term divorced friend, now an empty-nester:

Treat your leisure calendar as you would a job. Fill the blanks and ensure there is always something on the horizon to look forward to. The early days are the hardest and that is when you should remain the busiest. Eventually a routine rhythm appears and a new normal emerges.

Finding yourself alone can also be an opportunity to start to explore those things that you put off or never had time for. If you have friends in your orbit newly 'living alone', rally around joint friends to work together to keep their schedules full. If you are the solo dweller, reach out to your network to let them know you would appreciate their support during this time.

Sex in Mid-Life

I'll have what she's having.

– Nora Ephron

Or Not …

Oh, a blank page on sex? How delightfully provocative. Given my propensity to (over) share, you'd be forgiven for expecting a diary entry recounting wild affairs, a litany of past indiscretions, or perhaps the decades of 'mummy and daddy' time with the ever-present risk of little ones banging on the door.

Let's pause and ponder: what does sex mean now, in this grand mid of life?

I won't offer you sage wisdom on mid-life sexuality. Why? Because *you* are the author of your own erotic novella. Some may rekindle their nocturnal passions with new fervour while others – battle-worn – may relegate intimacy to birthdays and special occasions. Maybe sex was never a big part of your life, and now it's what you seek. Maybe celibacy is your new best friend.

The crux? Decipher your own desires. Open for business or closed for renovations – many will have opinions, but I say: dismiss them all. This is about *your* body, *your* needs, *your* comfort, and *your* interest. Whatever you choose, it's gloriously, unequivocally yours.

The Menopause Effect

Hormonal shifts and bone-aching exhaustion can make intimacy feel like a distant memory. The truth is menopause can significantly impact libido, comfort, and pleasure. Data shows that nearly 50% of postmenopausal women report issues with sexual function, yet this doesn't have to mean the end of desire – it just might look a little different.

PS If lack of desire, discomfort, or questions with no clear answers are bugging you, don't remain silent. Help is out there, so make sure to seek a professional's advice if needed. Your mid-life should be filled with joy – however that looks for you.

Feeling Connected – Your Later-in-Life Tribe

Diary Note …

Those '18 homes' by my 21st birthday also meant I attended five high schools – Dad had an appetite for new horizons. This nomadic lifestyle was a double-edged sword: it fostered resilience and introduced a love of wanderlust and the thrill of a new place – but conversely, a perpetual sense of rootlessness. A handful of long-term relationships have survived the decades – these women are magnificent and magnanimous in their understanding; sometimes years pass between visits. The best of relationships can just pick up where you last left them, love and respect a constant. Then there are the drains. Growing up amidst constant change blessed me with a top-notch 'bullshit detector', allowing me to swiftly distinguish between those who spark joy and those who need to be thanked for their services and shown the door.

We've examined that mid-life brings with it a curious paradox: the push and pull of stability versus change. At a time when we might expect to settle into familiar patterns, mid-life often nudges us toward reinvention – whether we expect it or not. As we evolve, so do our social circles. Relocation, a shift in career, or a major life event can leave us facing the possibility of isolation, yet there's something liberating in the opportunity to redefine our circles. The truth lies in having people in your orbit for 'a reason, a season, or a lifetime'. 'Forever friends' remain one of the most precious. Forging new connections is equally delightful.

Your Tribe Vibe

Studies now show that having a close-knit community – one you truly call your tribe – is one of the most important determinants of healthy longevity. In Okinawa (one of the Blue Zones) it is tradition for baby girls to be assigned to a group of four other baby girls upon birth, a *moai*. This is a 'special support group' for social, financial, spiritual, and health support – as quoted by a 77-year-old Okinawan woman,

Each member knows that her friends count on her as much as she counts on her friends. If you get sick or a spouse dies or if you run out of money, we know someone will step in and help. It's much easier to go through life knowing there is a safety net.

Imagine the peace of knowing that no matter what life throws at you, there are friends always there to catch you. Mid-life offers the perfect time to create a support posse of our own.

In the West, we have more fractured families and structures, so familial relationships may be challenging. Friendships and community need to be nurtured – during rosy times and, even more so, through life's tougher seasons.

Connection isn't something that happens passively – it's an intentional practice. Whether through a shared interest, a common goal, or even a fleeting conversation in a café, forging new friendships is both an art and a necessity. Connection makes the world go round.

Should You Be Bidding Toodle-oo to Anyone?

We all have off days, even besties. Keep them close and work through hiccups. However (and this might be an 'ouch' moment), who in your life no longer brings you joy? It's not about casting people aside in haste but recognising when a relationship has run its course. We grow, change, and, sometimes, outgrow people. As much as it hurts, some relationships simply reach their natural end. The focus becomes seeking a tribe that nourishes.

When Family Ties Fray

Family relationships, however, are a different beast entirely. Estrangement, though painful, is more common than we'd like to admit. Whether it's parents and children growing distant, siblings at odds, or unresolved tensions with in-laws, we often expect family to be our emotional bedrock. Yet sometimes, that foundation can crumble, leaving a gaping void.

I've seen it firsthand: the mother-in-law passing without reconciling with her son, adult children cutting ties with their parents. Expectations often play a role, or little misunderstandings snowball over time. Acceptance doesn't mean giving up; it's understanding that peace can come from letting go. Rather than mourning what could have been, we shift our focus to relationships that bring comfort and joy.

Sometimes, the family we choose – our close friends, partners, even mentors – becomes more nurturing than the one we're born into. There's power in surrounding yourself with people who nourish your spirit. These are the relationships that act as emotional life rafts, steadying us when we feel untethered. Only you know who should be in your life.

You'll have noticed more than a rosy passing mention of my family members – so, lest you think *it's fine for her*, I should point out that we are not the Waltons. On any given day, at least one family member manages to irritate me sideways – a sentiment I know is mutual. Decades ago, I decided if familial transgressions are more clueless than malicious, they're not reason enough to sever ties. I get more joy with my family in my life than I'd get without, so we muddle along tolerating each other's foibles and try not to step on too many toes in return. There's little they could do these days to truly make me walk away – forever's a long time, after all. My sisters and I have tittered over many a late-night phone call, trading *bons mots* about some of our parents' more memorable moves. And no doubt, our kids will probably do the same about us. That's the trick, isn't it? Family isn't about an endless supply of

Memorably, I once accidentally sent a text about Mum to Mum – it was intended for a sister to read, so not ideal.

My parents are divorced, and both my husband and I have a sibling we don't much keep up with.

sweetness and harmony but finding that workable mix of love and tolerance, peppered with the grace to let some things slide.

Take Action or Move On

Regrets 'at the end' for things you haven't done extend to exchanges with others you wish you might have handled differently – if you had time over. If not addressing 'skeletons' continues to plague you, I suggest a couple of choices.

1. If your perceived 'wrong' can be 'righted', making peace, take action. Call the person, have an honest talk, write a letter, apologise, whatever approach feels right for you. Be prepared to be met with a less-than-positive response. Stick to a heartfelt script. Deliver, then move on.

2. If, for whatever reason, the situation is unsalvageable, or you cannot cope with opening old wounds – seek professional assistance if it remains a block to your future joy. What is done is done. Let go.

TRY THIS

With old friends, book an annual trip around a shared friend anniversary, for example, the date kids started or left school. Take turns picking the destination and prepare to have adventures together. connect intentionally.: Reach out to former colleagues, old schoolmates, or friends you haven't spoken to in a while – sometimes, the best relationships are rekindled ones.

It may seem harder in mid-life to meet folk – here are a few spots you might happen upon your 'new' now tribe.

1. **Join a local club or class.** From fitness groups to art workshops, regular meet-ups around a common interest are perfect for cultivating new friendships.

2. **Host a gathering.** Invite a few acquaintances over for a casual dinner or a weekend hike and ask everyone to bring a friend. Expanding your circle.

3. **Volunteer in your community.** Giving back is a fulfilling way to meet new people while contributing positively

By taking a few deliberate actions, you can surround yourself with people who support and inspire you.

Navigating a (Still) Full House

Hello and help! Our house, which once felt perfectly fine for a young family, has required some serious adjusting now that we have kidults in the mix. If I'm honest, part of my consternation – and a significant driver for my 'fleeing' from home – was the full nest. Born from the chaos of COVID homeschooling, a husband working from home, and a house that heaved with the human (and furry) kind, I had an eye on the finish line that never quite materialised. I didn't wish my sons out, except – and I know I'm not alone – I didn't imagine my second act would involve evening meals and unloading the dishwasher.

In the 'olden days', the ink had barely dried on our high school certificate before my sisters and I were out of the family home –

off to uni, flatting, or travelling. To be fair, I did boomerang back a couple of times, but it was always temporary. My husband had a similar experience, returning home briefly for further study. Now recent reports suggest that we're likely to see a significant rise in adults over 40 still living at home, driven by soaring living costs and changing family dynamics.

The Kidults

Our offspring remaining in their childhood bedrooms longer than we expected is, for them, a mix of gratitude and frustration, a tug-of-war between their need for independence and the realities of living costs that keep them tethered. This shift requires a delicate dance between independence and connection.

It's not that they don't want to leave – believe me, they would love nothing more. But the crux is that we want them to save for a good start when they eventually move on. So, for now, we're all in this together.

A Balancing Act

Parents often find themselves juggling their own mid-life aspirations with the needs of their adult offspring. Making it work requires clear boundaries, open communication, and a hefty dose of patience. It's about finding that sweet spot where everyone's needs are met or, at least, acknowledged.

This means renegotiating house rules, discussing financial contributions, and respecting each other's privacy and independence within the shared space.

The blue sky in all this is becoming 'friends' – closer family connections and mutual support, provided everyone remains flexible and understanding. I don't have all the answers, but after two years, we've settled into a rhythm. When we are together, it's lovely. Travelling and celebrating milestones, I secretly feel blessed to have my 'babies' longer. We might still argue about who does what around the house – but less and less.

TRY THIS

Our household survives with a little forward planning – several months a year, we aim to have one fewer family member 'in situ'. Hubby goes golfing with friends, I disappear to our North Queensland abode, one or both of the young adults go away on a long weekend or extended trip with mates. Creating breathing room for all.

My Parenting Advice?

Well, it runs to – I have none. There are bits I've done well and bits I've screwed up – all in the rearview mirror (yes, more 'car talk').

Moving forward however my advice runs to; proffering 'life instructions' to your kidults becomes white noise as they move into adulthood and find their own way. To this point, I read this gem somewhere recently – goodness knows where or I would attribute it – the concept of WAIT: why am I talking?

My take? Add the S, WAIST: why am I *still* talking?

Go give those young adults in your orbit a HUGE hug – life is a little daunting when the apron strings are snipped. They don't need our advice. Our love will do the job. Retrospective parenting is pointless. Besides, isn't that what grandchildren are for? Practise on our own kids so we can get it right with the grandbabies!

… And Then They Are Really Grown

Anyone else recall stating loudly, 'I am your parent, not your friend'? Well, now you can be a wise, kindly, guiding friend.

Diary Note …

You wish for more time, alone. A soupçon of space to gather your thoughts. It's delivered, all the hours you want, for you. Then for all the world you don't want it so much anymore. You want time back, with your babies. My mother-in-law bailed me up mid-moan during the toddler years, 'Be careful,' she cautioned. 'The time goes quickly, then they are gone.' Yeah well, as I attempted to release the little hand in a limpet-like grip on my ankle, I probably told her to 'please be VERY quiet' (or a variation of …). She is gone, along with that time. I wish I could tell her I now know she was right.

Are these reflections a contradiction? Given I've suggested you pop yourself frontline and centre – A Grown Up's Gap Year – absolutely not. The biggest conundrum of all: nothing is as all-consuming, as fierce, or as everlasting as the love of a child. But it's inevitable that at some point time will free up – we have taken the steps together so you might put yourself in a position where you have something sorted to fill a void, feel better about the transitions.

Navigating the Empty Nest

As I still live with a full house, I asked a couple of my empty-nester friends for their thoughts:

One shared,

I alternated between sobbing and celebration for months. On one hand, I love the peace and freedom – a full fridge, moving my office out of the cupboard into a spare bedroom, an empty washing basket. But I keep waiting for the front door to swing open, for the laughter and the stomp of young men's sneakers.

Another added, 'After a month of mad organising, I decided to set up a weekly 'dinner at ours' night. Open to our kids and friends, it's become a new tradition. Now is the time to solidify friendships and plan a future for ourselves.'

The key? Be the place your children want to return to, without obligation. Think of a role in their lives that is uniquely yours. Oh, and let it all sit a bit before you go changing the locks – after all, they do come back, usually with laundry, or so I've heard.

The Joy Found in Lending a Hand

An earnest interest in fellow humans and a heart generous in spirit are the cornerstones of a life well-lived. Living in a privileged society lots of the best things in life are, if not free, then readily accessible – great health care, nutrition, education, safe environments. Should you live in good fortune, I feel passionately that we must aim (to the best of our circumstances) to live in optimum health, so we might have the energy to lend a hand.

How can you contribute to the collective?

It needn't be elaborate. When my dad returned to live in his birth country after a sixty-year absence, he needed to rebuild a network of friends. He noticed the properties in his street were looking neglected, and many of the now elderly neighbours didn't speak to each other. He began by organising a neighbourhood clean-up committee – those who could help visited their less able neighbours. They just celebrated ten years of 'friendly neighbours' with a street party. The area is blooming with fresh gardens, sparkling windows, and a celebration of all the local families at Christmas. From small things …

Mentoring. Sharing your knowledge with those just starting out or navigating a new path can be incredibly fulfilling. You could offer mentorship within your industry or volunteer with local programs to guide youth, women re-entering the workforce, or community groups.

Support for migrants. From offering language support to sharing cultural insights, there are organisations that need volunteers to make new arrivals feel more at home and connected.

Reading in schools. Volunteer as a reading buddy or literacy mentor in local schools. Programs like these not only support children's literacy development but also foster a love for learning.

Angel-investing in purpose-driven ventures. Support early-stage businesses or social enterprises that align with your values. By becoming an angel investor, you could help shape the future of purpose-driven companies while providing invaluable guidance.

Purposeful choices in mid-life not only give back, but they also add a meaningful dimension to this stage of life.

TRY THIS

A seat at the table. Joining the board of a charity or cause that's close to your heart is a way to lend your experience, voice, and decision-making to something that matters.

The Elixir of Youth – Never Stop Learning, Never

If you don't learn constantly, you don't grow, and you will wither. Too many people wither on the vine. Sure, it gets a little harder as you get older, but new experiences and new challenges keep it fresh.

– Iris Apfel

Diary Note …

A steadfast willingness to consistently move forward is a trait I'm swiftly discovering becomes more challenging as time marches on. Yet, it's also the very thing that keeps us vibrant, engaged, and dare I say, relevant.

Withering on the vine? Not on my watch. This book is, after all, the antithesis of stagnation. It's about growth, exploration, and keeping that spark alive, no matter what age you are. At some stage, you might no longer be required to front up for scheduled paid work – for some that will be sweet freedom, for others, incredibly daunting. We have already chatted about how ageing in joy and health requires more than just a sunny disposition. It requires purpose. Maintaining a reason to get out of bed every

day will be key to not just surviving but thriving. Sure, a little time out to lie under a palm tree is lovely – 365 days a year of it, not so much.

The Act of Learning

Learning something new is like a shot of adrenaline to the soul. Neuroscientists have found that engaging in lifelong learning doesn't only make us more knowledgeable, but it also helps maintain cognitive function as we age. Studies consistently show that adults who regularly challenge their minds with new skills or information tend to have better memory, increased attention span, and improved problem-solving abilities while also experiencing greater life satisfaction and mental wellbeing.

For me, continuing to learn isn't just about adding new skills to the repertoire (though that's a nice bonus). It's about staying curious and engaged with the world. It's about having something to look forward to, something that makes me feel alive.

Take a moment to think about the last time you learned something new. Did it make you feel more awake and connected to the world around you? That's the magic. It's not just about the knowledge itself, but the process – the challenge, the discovery, the joy of not knowing and then, suddenly, knowing.

Follow Your Curiosity

The beauty of mid-life is that we get to choose what we learn. No longer bound by school curriculums or the pressures of early career building, we can follow our interests wherever they lead. Want to learn how to play the piano? Go for it. Curious about astrophysics? There's a class for that.

So, let's make a pact: never stop learning. Never. Keep reading, keep exploring, keep asking questions. Stay curious, stay engaged, and stay young at heart. Because the elixir of youth isn't found in a bottle or a pill – it's found in the pursuit of something more.

Breakout

Never Too Late

Heather Cornish is a longtime friend and ex-work colleague. When I heard on the grapevine she had enrolled in uni – in an entirely new profession, in her late fifties – well, of course I knew we needed to hear about her experiences.

'When COVID hit, my role was made redundant. Not only that, my husband, German and an only child, had escaped the first lockdown to check on his parents, only to realise he couldn't leave them as they were no longer capable of living alone. Whilst I loved my marketing career, I felt burned out and yearned for something new. So, I decided to move to Germany to be with my husband and help care for his parents.

'I decided to fill my days studying a long-held interest: psychology. Of course, as I embarked on this, top of mind was *oh my god – can I even do this at my age?* It's 30 years since I was last at uni.

'I pushed through self-doubt by applying myself. As a mature student, all the learnings from a challenging career came to the fore, so this time around I had more discipline, planned better, felt more focused, and was better able to anticipate what was required.'

Heather's Tips for Mid-Life Joy

- When you change careers, all of your existing skills and talents come with you – nothing is lost.

- Staying flexible is helpful – I have relocated to Germany and reinvented my life from scratch, none of which was planned.

- Make the most out of wherever you are – with all of Europe on my doorstep, mini breaks are great fun, and I have the best little black book of travel tips now!

Heather Cornish has had a career in marketing and branding, working in eight countries. She is now completing a Master of Arts in psychology – and volunteering with the homeless. Embodying reinvigoration in mid-life.

An Open Mind is Interesting and Engaging

Travel is the great expander. Travelling well has you keeping your eyes open, options fluid, preconceived ideas to one side. I thought I had all this in the bag … thinking not the same as doing, as I was reminded.

A Grown Up's Gap Trip Diary Note …

I was the only person in the seaside Croatian town wearing a one-piece swimsuit as I continue to give too much of a damn about looser skin, my middle-aged body, blah, blah – this morning I'd had enough of my attitude. Now I'm reclining poolside in a bikini with just enough fabric to keep my butt covered. A string bikini is a shade too far. Still, I'm evolving – and keeping an open mind.

Do You Want to Be the Engaging Woman in the Room? I Do …

Think for a moment about the people who draw you in with their vitality and engagement, an open mind sitting high on the list of desirable traits – a willingness to dig deeper than a social media soundbite on an issue that may intrinsically sit on an opposing side of the fence from their beliefs in order to (now, this is the clincher) allow space for another's opinion.

Designing a lifestyle where you remain relevant and engaging won't ward off getting older – that is a certainty on the calendar, and yet having an open mind does not discriminate with age – my 83-year-old father is a lifelong adopter of the zeitgeist. Whatever is a leap forward, he is on it – collecting 'new' ways of viewing the world. Life is a wavy line of differing circumstances and comfort zones. A delightful sideline of mid-life is more time to be able to absorb the many shapes of humankind – less chasing our tail and more sitting to really listen, observe, and yes, evolve. With this, a desire to try new things, new ways, perhaps adopting a different perspective.

TRY THIS

Finding a role model to emulate is a great place to start. Without too much thought, who pops into your head as an invigorating, interesting, open-minded What inspires you about this person? This brings me to (in case I forget to mention this later) **laughter**.

Laughter is the best medicine.

Laugh. Often. At yourself, a situation. Laugh with others. When things seem dire it may be hard to find 'funny' – yet these times may seem lighter and easier to navigate if you look at it all from a sense of abstract humour. Along the lines of…you can't make this shit up! Because sometimes truth is stranger than fiction.

Career in Mid-Life

In the 1980s, the phrase 'having it all' became a rallying cry for women entering the workforce in unprecedented numbers. Fast forward to today, and we're witnessing a new revolution: the rise of the mid-life career pivot.

My own journey reflects this trend. My corporate management career ended when I became 'mummy on deck' – a role that plugged the gap for twenty years. Around twelve months into my tenure as 'full-time mum', I was not entirely satisfied with being tied to the dishwasher or tuckshop. I used the in-between hours to study, retrain, upskill, and expand horizons. Clinical nutritionist, fitness trainer, Kids Food School founder, organic baking business, stylist, travel writer, travel website editor, fashion designer, lifestyle and interiors contributing editor, fiction writing diploma, finance recruitment, law student, health and wellness coach, Mandarin lessons, Japanese lessons –evidently, I didn't subscribe to the sage advice to 'stick to your lane'. A move I once viewed as a misstep had become a strength. My choices widened as I navigated my next stage of working life.

This patchwork of experiences isn't uncommon. According to a 2020 LinkedIn survey, the average person changes jobs 12 times during their career. For women, especially those who've taken career breaks, these transitions often cluster in mid-life.

I now see mid-life women with energy and inclination and nowhere to take it. Many of our cohort would gladly pick up the slack for younger women wanting their turn to step away to raise families. The equation is wrong. Good women will continue to slip through the net, and as an ageing population with a social construct to maintain, we need all hands on deck. Most wouldn't argue professional purpose is a key indicator of longevity – paid, volunteer, philanthropic, what have you – engagement the goal. Choice the key.

Casting the Net

When I wanted to re-enter the workforce, I was 54 years old. Despite deciding I was going to be scrutinised as 'too old', even with my breadth and depth of experience – some of it recent and relevant to many roles that interested me – I started applying randomly. Not much doing, then I thought *bugger it* and went rogue. Going back to finish my law degree wasn't going to 'complete' me, but two years back at uni and I could make peace with this. On and on, trying this and that on for size, I received the ultimate reward for my efforts: the confidence from being re-engaged soon sparked other opportunities, and these 'light me up'.

My experience aligns with research from the *Harvard Business Review*, which found that older workers bring valuable soft skills to the table – emotional stability, complex problem-solving, and nuanced decision-making. These attributes, honed through years of life experience, are increasingly valued in today's workplace.

The lesson is to go wide, out to old professional contacts, play to your strengths, upskill, grow a thick skin, and realise your worth (mid-life women make exemplary employees) – stare down any impostor syndrome fears and go for it.

TRY THIS

When you flounder, ask yourself, *What did I never do that I wished I had?* – it matters not whether, on paper, your experience seems to correlate. It could transpire the wackier the better – because, as we have discussed, we don't want to die wondering. Update your LinkedIn profile, join a professional women's group. if you want to start a small business, take a look at government resources. Often, state governments offer 'back to work grants' for women re-entering the workforce (covering training contribution and other costs). Sign up for alerts when applications open.

Rebranding and Pivoting with Michelle B Griffin

As I navigated my own re-entry into corporate life, I was fortunate to have Michelle as a business mentor. Her insights were invaluable, helping me see the potential in my diverse experiences. Michelle's own journey of transformation resonated deeply, and I knew her story could inspire others facing similar crossroads.

Michelle B Griffin exudes an energy that's invigorating. She is the embodiment of her own philosophy: that mid-life is the perfect time to bet on yourself.

'The years have made us wiser, not older,' Michelle tells me, her eyes twinkling with the excitement of someone who's found their true calling. 'So, the time to seize life is now! Four years ago, I 'rewrote my trajectory' by launching this consultancy. It was a dream in my twenties, but life and circumstances led me – or perhaps held me – to what I now realise was the 'right for me' moment. I'm more equipped now. Back then, it was for show; now, it's about impact. It's deeper and more meaningful. I'm thankful for the lessons that wisdom taught me.'

Michelle's work through her company, Standout Women, reflects this depth. She sees a common thread among mid-life women ready to bet on themselves. They've made 'the great leap', only to find themselves grappling with fundamental questions:

'Who am I? What is 'it' that I want?'

'The irony is,' Michelle says, 'the answers are already within you. You must find out who you are, not what you do. Life can erase our identity if we let it.'

As our conversation winds down, Michelle shares her tips for women looking to 'own their lane'. 'The answers come when we get out of our heads and into conversations. Perhaps mid-life is not a rewrite but a redirect to where we're meant to be at this season. This applies to a later in life career transition AND life in general.'

Sometimes, the most fulfilling chapters begin right in the middle.

Michelle B Griffin is a speaker, author, and founder of Standout Women Media, empowering professionals, especially women in business, to 'Own Your Lane' with personal branding for impact, opportunity, and growth.

Shez Ford: Busy Professional with Heart

Shez and I share a connection as school mums. For years, I watched her career soar from afar, wondering, *How can she do it all?*

Shez Ford, a senior executive in global financial services, exudes warmth and authenticity. Her dedication to helping others achieve their potential is evident.

'To achieve personal and professional fulfilment,' Shez begins with a smile, 'I draw on the deeply ingrained principles from my cultural background – I'm Sri Lankan – and my family upbringing.'

Take the free online survey the Sparktype Test, a useful tool to identify your strengths personally and professionally.

'First, don't take yourself too seriously. Second, be real – authentic – and prioritise your wellbeing and joy. Third, don't be afraid to display humility and generosity. My grandmother always said that the true sign of a great human is one who can comfortably engage with anyone, be it the poorest person in the village or royalty, and put people at ease through empathy.'

'And finally, respect, love and grow your village – you get out of life what you put in. Community is everything – on the home and work front.'

LinkedIn is where it is at for a career reboot resource. Michelle has co-authored *The LinkedIn Branding Book* and co-hosts a podcast.

As our conversation deepens, Shez shares how becoming a parent prompted her to reassess her priorities. 'When I had kids, I had to reset my life and attach myself back to my core principles. That meant reframing what 'good' looked like for me both personally and professionally. I learnt that it was less about what I did and more about the impact I had on others' lives.'

She continues, her tone resolute, 'I got clear about my non-negotiables. The responsibility of parenthood meant I needed to allow myself to be 'me', not a crowd-pleaser. This realisation brought simplicity to my life. I knew I needed to work at being a great wife, mum, daughter, friend. My husband and I discussed our priorities and implemented arrangements that meant our kids were well looked after, so we could enjoy what is important to us.'

Shez's story reminds me that there's no one-size-fits-all approach to balancing career and family. We may take different paths, but the key is to prioritise what truly matters to us.

Shez Ford is a senior executive in global financial services, dedicated to helping others achieve their potential. Balancing career and personal life with clear non-negotiables, Shez prioritises family, wellbeing, and joy.

AUTUMN POSSIBILITIES

As you bring the 'Autumn – Feel Connected' section to a close, reflect on the opportunities this season offers for deepening your sense of connection and fulfilment. Here's how the chapters guided you through this transformative time:

1. **Embracing connection and community.** Whether it's with your later-in-life tribe, navigating a still-full house, or finding joy in lending a hand, spend Autumn feeling truly connected.

    TRY THIS

    Today call a friend you haven't seen in a while – set up a FIRM time to meet for a walk and coffee.

2. **Navigating life's transitions.** Evolving dynamics of mid-life relationships, loss, and discovery.

    TRY THIS

    If you need support navigating a recent life transition, schedule an appointment this week with a coach, therapist, or mentor – empower yourself to move forward with confidence.

3. **Pursuing lifelong growth and learning.** Never stop learning and keep an open mind – the elixir of youth.

TRY THIS

Think of three people you trust who could offer guidance as you explore career or personal transitions. Send each one an email this week to reconnect and ask them for a coffee to discuss your ideas and get their input.

4. **Choosing a beautiful life amidst challenges.** Life isn't without its lemons, but Autumn encourages you to remember that, even in the face of challenges, your life can be full of joy, meaning, and fulfilment.

TRY THIS

Celebrate this vibrant phase of life by booking a professional photoshoot. Capture your midlife confidence and sense of freedom.

5. **Rediscovering the treasures close to home.** As you journey through Autumn, you'll find that the greatest treasures often lie right in your backyard.

TRY THIS

How can you contribute locally? Connect within your community and commit to exploring options within the next two weeks.

Autumn is a time to settle into the life you've designed – to deepen your relationships, embrace new possibilities, and truly thrive in this fulfilling stage of life.

DESTINATION
YOUR MID-LIFE

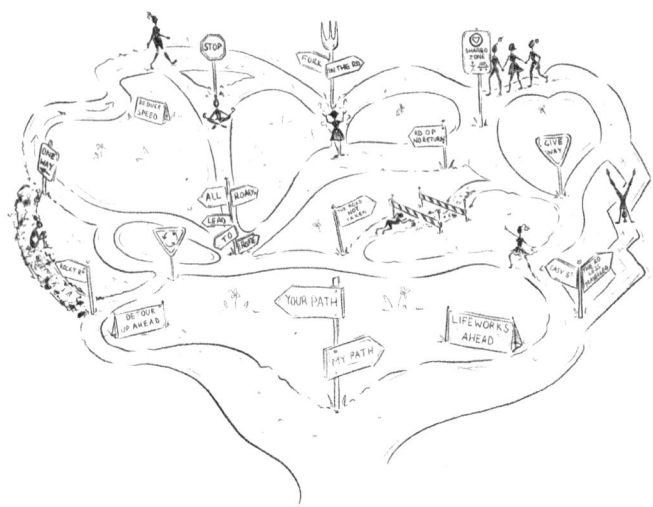

There is No One Path, Several Lessons Here

My late mother-in-law Norma and I shared a love of her son, grandsons, and each other – and sometimes, it felt like not much else. She was perfectly content at home, surrounded by the familiar, once declaring holidays and travel as 'pointless' (and you now know how much they spark my energy). Her choice – a contained life. My choice – a 'wild ride'.

Several months before her passing, my 'other mum' resided in a home that didn't even faintly resemble the *Best Exotic Marigold Hotel* version I imagined for my future. During one visit, I spoon-fed her, feeling acutely the circle of life – her 95 years to my 55.

Naively, I'd always thought she was doing 'living wrong' – never seeking novelty but rather comfort in the familiar. 'Book a trip' I urged her when her husband passed. When eventually I became so frustrated by her lack of expansiveness I booked her on a cruise. The day of departure, her (packed by me) suitcase sat resolutely outside her front door as the ship set sail without her. She had told me she was perfectly happy with her lot – I chose not to listen.

And, dear reader, that's the whole point. She showed me there's no best path – just the one that feels right for you. Your 'beautiful' life, your way.

Choosing a Beautiful Life

Life can be beautiful if you make it beautiful.

– Eddie Jaku, age 101

There's a particular kind of magic in meeting someone who embodies the very essence of resilience and joy. Mr Eddie Jaku (may he rest in peace) was one such enchanting soul. When I had the opportunity to hear him speak, he was a newly minted author at the sprightly age of 100. He bounded onto the stage with an energy that made a mockery of his centenarian status. For thirty mesmerising minutes, he held a packed auditorium in thrall, his vitality a vivid testament to his message.

Later, as he signed books, he gifted each reader a precious moment of connection. My then-16-year-old son stood before this Holocaust survivor, this beacon of hope, absorbing a lesson more powerful than any classroom could provide. Mr Jaku's most poignant teaching? Despite life's cruel curve balls, the power to shape our destiny lies within our grasp. YOU can choose responsibility for your life outcomes. Just pick your version, and make it happen.

TRY THIS

Read Mr Jaku's book *The Happiest Man on Earth.*

Michael McHugh and How Women Help Shape Good Men

I've known Michael McHugh for around 17 years – first as a fellow school parent with his wife Michelle (our sons were in the same class), then briefly as my editor at *MiNDFOOD* magazine, and finally as the artist behind one of my most treasured artworks. Over the years, I've watched Michael's ability to understand and collaborate with women, both personally and professionally. Whether as editor-in-chief guiding his predominantly female team at *MiNDFOOD*, writing for his female readership, or working with Michelle and their two daughters, Michael's natural empathy and insight are undeniable.

It's no surprise, then, the strong influence of his mother runs through everything he does, as is evident in his story:

'In the September 2018 edition of our *MiNDFOOD* magazine, we created an issue celebrating the suffragette movement. That issue was also a time for reflection, as my mother had just passed away at the age of 95. When Monique asked me to write something about the women in my life who have shaped my thinking, I remembered this editorial. It's my mother who had the greatest impact on the boy I was and the man I became.

'Mum had that knack, as supportive parents do, of loving unconditionally and allowing me to think that anything was possible. If I ever felt down or blue, it was Mum who would point out the brighter side of life. She taught me resilience, to see the good in people, and to feel the importance of family. She was intelligent and I can only imagine what she would have gone on and done today with all the different options now available to women leaving school, as her grandchildren today are doing extraordinary things.

'I felt so much love from Mum. She instilled in me many things and shaped the way I see the world. In lots of ways, she was the suffrage light in my life, guiding and encouraging me along, supporting and shining the path of what my life could be like. When she passed, it profoundly affected me. I had always painted, studied art and design, but when I started *MiNDFOOD*, I put my painting to one side. Mum's passing reignited something within me. I attended an 8-week masterclass of painting at the National Art School. From there, things took off with sell-out exhibitions. It's a wonderful thing, later in life, to experience reinvigoration and fulfilment. It's never too late.

'I miss my mother and that sense of light alongside me. The power of a wonderful woman, whom I loved very much, those women who have gone before and lit a path for us all to learn from are all worth celebrating. Thanks, Mum.'

Michael McHugh is an artist and editor-in-chief of MiNDFOOD *magazine, combining his passion for creativity with editorial work. After years focused on his magazine, the loss of his mother reignited his love for painting. Now, Michael paints daily, inspiring through his art.*

TRY THIS

Consider writing your eulogy now. What legacy would the future you wish to leave your loved ones, the world?

A Final Word: Making the Most of Life's Opportunities

At 77, my mum, or Connie (Cornelia), as the world knows her, radiates vibrancy, a joy for life that permeates even the smallest conversations. We sit side by side at our favourite spot, the small beachside café overlooking Sydney Harbour. The sun catches the glimmer of the ocean pool where we have our weekly swim, saltwater still fresh on our skin. Mum sips her coffee (always long black), glancing at the waves as they roll in. She's always been at home near the water.

'Do you ever think about everything you've accomplished?' I ask. 'You've done so much, Mum.'

'I never saw it that way,' she says. 'There wasn't time to think about it. There's always something new to do.'

Her life reads like a novel – one that could easily be shelved in the adventure section. Her choices were bold, often unorthodox, and always a little ahead of their time. Yet, she doesn't see herself that way. It's how she's always approached life: without fanfare, moving forward with grace, no matter what. This was the woman who built a skiwear company and later a real estate business, who was the first female auctioneer and zone chairperson in the region. And as if that wasn't enough, she got her British naval deep-sea diving qualifications – something I still can't quite believe – in the pitch black of the ocean while sharks swam past her. She never hesitated. She simply pressed on, exploring a world few would dare enter.

'That's what life is, Monique. You dive in.'

'You were fearless,' I add.

She laughs, shaking her head. 'I wasn't fearless. I just didn't know how to stop.'

For her, it was never about chasing accolades or recognition, instead showing that strength comes from constantly reinventing oneself, from understanding that life rolls, and the only thing to do is roll with it. My boys – her grandsons – may never know the woman who once swam with sharks or skied black runs, but they will always see the legacy she passed down.

'It wasn't always easy,' she admits. 'But you push through. You don't sit and dwell. If I could give advice to my younger self, it would be: if it feels good, do it. Don't overthink things. There's no time to waste.'

And there it is – the heart of my mother's wisdom. She taught me that life doesn't always come with a map, but if you keep moving, keep a positive attitude, keep believing in yourself, keep saying yes to the next step – the path will reveal itself.

As we sit looking out over the water, I realise that this is my love letter to her – a testament to all she's taught me. And if my boys can see me as the role model she's been to me, then maybe that's the best legacy I could ever hope to leave.

Cornelia 'Connie' van Tulder is a pioneering entrepreneur, real estate professional, and adventurer (and mum to my sisters and me). From building a skiwear company to earning deep-sea diving qualifications, her resilience and curiosity have been lifelong companions – continually inspiring with a zest for life and unwavering belief in seizing opportunity.

And so, I dedicate this chapter to my mum, to all mums, all women who care, are carers, and to the carers who came before and will come after. Life may indeed serve up lemons from time to time, but the choice to find beauty, adventure, and joy in the moments – that choice is ours to make.

The Treasure in Your Backyard

Now that you've read – and hopefully worked your way through – *A Grown Up's Gap Year*, I imagine you've come to the same conclusions I did: the life you lead can be by design; it's never too late, and the groundwork you lay matters. Every day is a gift, and life should be fun, even if the journey gets bumpy.

Starting to make changes is hard. Staying the same, if you're unsatisfied, is harder. But here's the truth: you don't need grand gestures or overnight transformations to shift your life. Sometimes, the treasure isn't in far-off places or big changes – it's in your own backyard, waiting to be rediscovered.

Perhaps, all along, you've carried exactly what you need within you. Realising this is the first step. The second? Taking action. Even baby steps matter. They're all you need to begin.

It's empowering, isn't it? Knowing that the key to joy and fulfilment lies in the decisions you make, in the simple act of starting. Let tomorrow be the first morning you wake with anticipation – that eager kind, the one that propels you forward. Make your move. You're already equipped to take on whatever comes next. Don't stop laughing along the way. Be ever curious. Have a bloody good time with this one life. We're all ageing – let's make ours an interesting, healthy journey.

Don't let your epitaph read, *F**K, I forgot to live my life.*

Bon voyage, darling new friend – send me a postcard when you find your centre stage destination. I'd love to hear from you.

Wrapping Up A Grown Up's Gap Year

Daily Regime: Checklist: Your Guide To Feeling Better

Kind Start Morning
- ❑ Wake up & make bed
- ❑ Sunshine walk
- ❑ Regular Strength Training
- ❑ Hydrate & cold shower
- ❑ Dress to feel fabulous
- ❑ Oh, go on, light a little incense

Midday Momentum
- ❑ Real food lunch
- ❑ Mindful eating
- ❑ Move regularly during the day (3x10 mins)
- ❑ One act of joy

PM Regime
- ❑ Prep for tomorrow
- ❑ Limit screens
- ❑ Skincare & self-care

SLEEP SLAYER
- ❑ Create a calm sleep space
- ❑ Write it down; get any niggles out of your head and onto the page

The SPACE Method (Taking Action on a Grown-Up's Gap Year)

Simplify Your Lifestyle (Winter)

- ❑ Have you reinvigorated your wellbeing routine by decluttering your environment?
- ❑ Have you simplified your finances by sorting out your financial literacy?
- ❑ Have you simplified your daily routines, wardrobe, beauty routine, and home?
- ❑ Have you set clear boundaries on where to invest your time and energy?

Plan Your Mid-Life Project (YOU) (Winter/Spring)

- ❑ Have you taken stock of where you are in life and reviewed your backstory?
- ❑ Have you identified your core values and defined your second-act purpose?
- ❑ Have you designed a roadmap to guide the shape of your next life phase?
- ❑ Have you started building momentum and mental strength to move forward?
- ❑ Have you revived your mid-life mojo and sense of style?

Action Your Wellbeing (Spring/Summer)

- ❑ Have you checked off essential mid-life health tests and taken stock of your health?
- ❑ Are you fuelling your body with nutritious food and building firm healthy habits?

❑ Have you integrated strength training, movement, and fitness into your daily routine?

❑ Are you prioritising sleep, mindfulness, and mental health?

Connect With Your Tribe (Autumn)

❑ Have you curated your tribe – deciding who to keep close, who to distance from, and who to meet?

❑ Have you revisited your career path, explored new possibilities, or repurposed a new role that excites you?

❑ Have you consolidated your new lifestyle design for the future?

❑ Are you embracing love and joy in all its guises?

Explore Your Adventures (Summer/Autumn)

❑ Have you picked an adventure – a trip, event, or challenge – to ignite your sense of discovery and joy?

❑ Have you researched different options that fit your interests and budget?

❑ Are you exploring new activities and experiences that excite and fulfil you?

❑ Have you found the courage to be brave, try new things, and explore solo travel for self-discovery?

Remember, these prompts are meant to spark creativity, ponderance, and a smile. *A Grown Up's Gap Year* is your opportunity to reinvigorate your lifestyle, and enhance your wellbeing, sense of adventure, and chic. After all, this is **your** story, and it's time to prioritise **you**!

If All Else Fails ...

Bake a Pavlova!

Gather your loved ones, whip up this joyful dessert, and remind yourself that life's best moments are often simple. Pavlova is a triumph that takes all of 15 minutes to prepare. No special occasion needed – just because.

It's a gift to share, no fanfare required, and if there's one thing the world needs, it's a little more sweetness – no reservations, just life served à la meringue ...

For the base:

- 8 egg whites
- 250g caster sugar +
  250 gr brown sugar
  (I love the blend)
- 2 tsp cornflour
- 1 tsp white wine vinegar
- 1/2 tsp vanilla extract

For the topping:
- 650ml pure cream
- Mixed fresh fruit
  (passionfruit, berries,
  bananas, kiwi fruit, mango)

Method

Preheat the oven to 180°C. Line a baking sheet with baking paper and draw a rough oval – I use a favourite serving platter as a guide.

Whisk the egg whites until satiny peaks form, then whisk in the sugar, a tablespoonful at a time, until the meringue is stiff and shiny.

Sprinkle the cornflour, vinegar, and vanilla extract over the egg white, and fold in lightly with a metal spoon. Mound the meringue onto the baking paper and, using a spatula, flatten the top and smooth the sides.

Put in the oven and immediately reduce the heat to 120°C. Cook for an hour. Then turn off the oven and leave to cool completely.

Once it's cool, take the meringue disc out – and you can keep it in an airtight container for a couple of days or freeze for a month.

Whip the cream until thickened but still soft, and pile onto the meringue, spreading it to the edges. Add the fresh fruit. Voila – Joy on a platter.

Journal Prompts & Book Club Questions

The shape of your Grown Up's Gap Year will be entirely unique – let conversations and/or your pen flow, allowing the surprises to unfold. Use these prompts as springboards for inspiration, adventure, and joyful seeking. Remember, this is your journey – time to put you in the picture.

1. If you could design your ideal day, what would it look like from start to finish? Don't be stingy on dreaming – make this several pages of joy.

2. What's a skill you've always wanted to learn but haven't yet? Why not, now?

3. Recall a time when you stepped out of your comfort zone. What did you discover about your inner superwoman?

4. Identify five areas in your life – be they physical or emotional – that are overdue for a good clear-out. Embrace your inner minimalist and watch how a little simplification can make room for so much more. Write these down.

5. Describe a moment when you felt truly empowered. Was it when you finally mastered the art of saying 'no' without apologising?

6. What does 'putting yourself first' mean to you? Is it time to upgrade from supporting actor to centre stage in your own life?

7. Describe your perfect solo adventure. Where would you go? Why?

8. What's a childhood dream you've neglected? Is it time to revive that ambition?

Big Hugs and Thank You

Heartfelt thanks and appreciation to all my contributors featured in *A Grown Up's Gap Year* – your time, words of encouragement, and sharing your stories and wisdom made this book all the better.

Thank you to my husband, Michael, and sons B & H, you gave me the greatest gift of love – not chasing me down when I decided to flee temporarily and gentle acceptance when I arrived home. To my mum and dad, for your lifelong support – never questioning my moves, even when they were questionable. My sisters, Michelle for always encouraging me, and both of you for sweet childhood memories.

A heartfelt thank you to my editor, Melinda Louise Hutchings, for your steadfast belief in my project, your attention to detail, and professional organisation. A big thanks must also go to Virginia Lloyd, book coach; your guidance and professionalism early in this project propelled me to begin. To Michelle B Griffin – you 'untangled me' professionally; thank you. Liz Nable, your P.R guidance made sure my message didn't remain a secret, your assistance went well and beyond, thank you. To Sally-Ann Cowen, at my side with never-waning encouragement and full responsibility for my toned butt; thank you. Samantha McCarthy, travel colleague and friend – my 'Grown Up's Gap Year' was all the more fun with your professional care and kindness in my 'travel kit'.

To Emily Brown, you didn't simply give me the best haircut of my life, you quite literally 'recreated my life', thank you darling.

To Michael McHugh, your kindness and professional support has been invaluable, thank you. Jason Smith, publisher, you entered my orbit at precisely the right time – in 'taking my project on,' you made this journey complete, and I have a book I am proud of. Thank you. Finally, Madeleine Carroll, illustrator and friend, your patience, your interpretation of my ramblings, your talent, wit, and friendship gave life to these pages. Thank you, thank you!

Finally, to my Instagram community – without you, *A Grown Up's Gap Year* might have come and gone as a few journal entries. Your interest and support turned it into a book.

Illustrator

Madeleine Carroll joined this project during my 'dreaming stage', bringing it to life with her beautiful illustrations and captivating cover art. A joy to collaborate with, her gift lies in translating my creative vision into images that truly resonate. Based in Sydney, Madeleine is an innate creative being whose deft artistic talent shows no bounds. Be it illustration, couture design or even chocolate boxes, she blends whimsy and sophistication, telling stories that linger through her art.

Instagram: @madeleine.carroll

www.madeleinecarroll.com.au

CONTRIBUTORS

'I get by with a little help from my friends'
Professionals in their field, generously
sharing knowledge to enhance our
journey.

Ainslie Curran
Stylist, LoveDuck
Boutique.

Aisha Hillary-Morgan
Designer. Entrepreneur.
Experience Seeker.

Anna Manlulo
Filipino Food Movement.
Author.

Ayako Fukuda
Director of Wellness Six
Senses Kyoto.

Cornelia van Tulder
Entrepreneur.
Adventurer, My mum.

Desiree Prinsloo
Award-winning artist.
Reinvention.

Dr. Danielle Einstein, PhD
Clinical Psychologist.
Author.

Emily Brown
Entrepreneur.
Hairstylist.

Dr. Michele Squire, PhD
Scientist. Entrepreneur.
QR8 Skincare.

Heather Cornish
Marketing & branding
expert. Psychology.

Kate Kendall
Yogi & breathwork
facilitator. Flow Athletic

Lisa Jody Manser
Global Spa and Wellness
Director, COMO.

Lisa Walker
Co-founder, Eir Women.
Wellness.

Lissy Abrahams
Psychotherapist. Author.
Podcast host.

Liz Nable
Media & PR Expert.
Entrepreneur. Speaker.

Marie-Therese Hunter
Clinical Neurophysiology
Scientist. Swimmer.

Mary Delahunty
ASFA CEO.
Churchill Fellow.

Melissa Browne
Redefining wealth for
women. Author.

Melinda Louise Hutchings
Editor. Author. Marketing
& Comms Expert.

Michael McHugh
Editor-in-Chief
MiNDFOOD. Artist.

Michelle B Griffin
Speaker. Author.
Founder—Own Your Lane

Michelle Cox
Corporate leader. Author.
Creative entrepreneur.

Michelle van Tulder
Ex-finance director.
Property expert. Author.

Prue Francis
Agricultural consultant.
Catalyst for this book!

Sally-Ann Cowen
Expert. Excercise science,
nutrition, integrative health.

Sally Flegg
Photographer – natural
light headshots.

Shelly Horton
Journalist. National TV
presenter. Women's health.

Shez Ford
Senior Executive. Global
Financial Services.

Sophia Ivy Lee
Makeup artist. Natural,
flawless skin.

Vanessa Bell
Eco-entrepreneur. Merino
Wool. Podcast host.

Virginia Lloyd
Author. Book coach.
Publishing consultant.

About The Author

As a wellbeing advocate, nutritionist, travel and lifestyle writer, and mum with a mission, Monique van Tulder has spent decades encouraging women to feel better and 'go and explore'. Her latest project, A Grown Up's Gap Year, was born from her own twelve-month reinvigoration that led her to 'run away from her family' – then return to ask why so many second-act women feel compelled to 'power through', instead of 'put themselves in the picture'.

Based in Australia, between the harbourside city of Sydney (where her husband, two sons, mum, and sweet puppy hold down the fort) and tropical haven The Whitsundays. Monique writes with a light touch, even as she gets to the heart of what it means to truly live well. When she's not mapping out new possibilities, she is often somewhere interesting, asking herself, 'Why not ... now?'

Discover more of her work:
Website: moniquevantulder.com.au
Instagram: @moniquevantulder
Podcast: A Grown Up's Gap Year
Resources in this book can be found here:

Printed in Dunstable, United Kingdom